OUT of

The true story of an
Amish youth entangled
in the web of a cult

DECEPTION

OUT of

The true story of an
Amish youth entangled
in the web of a cult

DECEPTION

Nathan Miller

Ridgeway Publishing
Medina, New York

OUT OF DECEPTION

*To order additional copies
please visit your local
bookstore or contact:*

**Ridgeway Publishing
3129 Fruit Avenue
Medina, NY 14103
ph: 888.822.7894
fax: 585.798.9016**

Cover design by: M. Gagarin Design

ISBN# 978-0-9840985-3-8

Printed in the United States of America

Dedication

To my faithful wife Mattie and our precious children,
Sharon Marie, Martha Sue, and Emilee Hope.

And also to Wilbur and Joann Hochstetler
and their family.

Acknowledgments

Thank you, Wilbur and Joann. When you agreed to this project, you and I had no idea how tough it would be. This book really is our book, not my book. Wilbur, for sharing your heart. You spent many hours working on timelines, gathering information, interviewing, dredging up memories, adding here and changing there. None of this was easy, but you shared the vision of reaching others with your experiences. Your cooperation and dedication made this possible. And Joann, for your support and motivation. I'm sure it would have taken much longer and maybe even stopped altogether without your persistence. Your assistance in editing and critiquing was appreciated.

Thank you, Mattie, for providing loving support as only a wife can during the three years of working on this book. Your patience, commitment, and vision were critical factors in completing it. If readers see quality in here, it is because of your recurrent advice, "Now, take your time and do it right!"

Thank you, Norman Miller and the entire team at Ridgeway Publishing, for being the gears behind this book. Your tireless enthusiasm and encouragement were very important to us. You put in many hours of behind-the-scenes work to get this to the reader. Norman and Marlena, you even joined us on a retreat for a week to help work on it. What a blessing that was! The deadlines weren't exactly easy, but were important nonetheless. It takes a lot of organizing to publish a book.

Thank you, Kristy Wadsworth, for the hours you spent editing the manuscript. Your experience was a real blessing. Your encouragement, frank criticism, and challenging questions were invaluable. Your gift of taking a manuscript and making it readable really shone in this project. You made a great lead editor!

Thank you, Jacinto Yoder, for the hours you spent in the jungles of Nicaragua going through the manuscript with a fine-tooth comb, making sure all the i's were dotted and the t's were crossed. People enjoy reading a clean book. Copyediting is tedious, but someone has to do the dirty work, and you certainly did an outstanding job! You and Kristy made a great editing team!

Thank you to the Clarence Hochstetler family for sharing your stories and providing so many important details. You also spent many hours reviewing the manuscript. Your support was really appreciated.

— Nathan Miller

Foreword

Though *Out of Deception* is an unusual story, the locations, the people, and the experiences are real. It is an extraordinary tale, but the purpose in telling it is not entertainment. Nor is it to lift up some people while belittling others. The purpose is to point the reader to God.

The story is told through the eyes of Wilbur Hochstetler, known as Wil in the story. Many hours were spent interviewing Wil while he relived events and reconstructed details that happened more than twenty years ago. Others were also interviewed to insure accuracy and clarify details.

Undoubtedly, there are other perspectives. This book is about Wil's experiences and may not reflect those of the other members of Wilbur Lee Eash's group. Some things in this book may seem unbelievable, even bizarre. But they are true, nonetheless. In fact, some of the worst and weirdest incidents were left out. This book is an exposé of a searching heart gone awry, deceived and under Satan's control. Lest you think these were unusually ignorant or gullible people, they were not. They were normal people, just like you and me. No one deliberately becomes ensnared. "Let he who thinks he stands take heed, lest he fall."

Unfortunately, the greater part of this book is negative. Such entanglements, brainwashing, and devotion to a leader come gradually, while deliverance through Christ is simple and instant. Complete healing and changing of thought patterns take time, but salvation is immediate; hence, Wil's deliverance takes a much shorter section of the book.

Most of the names in this book, including Wil

Hochstetler and Wilbur Lee Eash, are real, though some writers' liberty has been taken to protect certain people's identities and privacy. Other details have been added to provide a backdrop for particular episodes. Conversations have been reconstructed as accurately as possible, although some have been created for flow and readability. The locations where the experiences took place are authentic. The settings, the people, and their actions have been kept as authentic as possible.

Our goal is to create an awareness of the dangers of cults and the potential of becoming thoroughly deceived when one is searching and looks in the wrong places. We also hope readers can learn to help those who may be ensnared as Wil was or who may be heading in that direction. May God receive all the glory.

— The Publishers

Table of Contents

Chapter 1

Meeting God

I ambled down the farm lane in search of solitude. The sun had already set, and a slight chill was in the air. An old barn came into view in the closing darkness, its graveled driveway overgrown with soft grass. Not knowing where else to go, I sank down on the step and leaned against the sturdy door frame. I bowed my head in my hands and heaved a deep, sad, lonely sigh.

Oh, for rest! For peace! my troubled soul agonized. *Where, oh, where is help for me?*

"What shall I do? Oh, what shall I do?" I cried aloud. I felt trapped. Caught. "If I stay, I'm ruined. If I leave, I'm ruined." My chest tightened as I weighed my desperate situation. *Where am I headed? Is there any hope? Is there a God? Is there really a God who loves me? If I only knew there was a God who loved me, it might help.* I sighed, utterly discouraged.

An owl hooted into the dark night. The lonely sound

echoed in my heart. I shivered. Lonely, depressed, and unloved. "What a joyless, purposeless existence," I moaned. "If I ever needed a sign, if I ever needed a God bigger than Wilbur Lee, it is right now."

I recalled that impious gleam in his dark brown eyes. My stomach turned. My body felt used, dirty, and drained. I was spent emotionally and physically. And I was only nineteen.

Suddenly, on impulse, I looked up into the clear star-spangled night sky. It was my moment, my decision, my destiny. My heart cried out in deepest desperation. *I have to know. I just have to know!* I tilted my head back, gazing at the stars, and cried, "If there is a God who loves me, show me!"

Flash! A meteorite blitzed across the black sky before my mouth had closed.

"Oh!" I whispered as my heart raced. "What did that mean?" I had prayed the most earnest, desperate prayer of my life, but I had not expected an answer so soon. I wasn't even sure whom I was praying to. *If there is a God who actually loves me, then I will find Him,* I determined.

As my pulse resumed its normal rate, I questioned what I had just seen. *Maybe I was too gullible,* I decided. *This will have to be tested. I'm not going to fall for something that will only take me down another discouraging and confusing path. I've had enough of that already . . .*

This is different though, I argued with myself. *But I have to know . . .*

I slowly turned my face heavenward once more. Ambivalent feelings of fear and hope surged through my questing soul. I voiced my simple petition a second time: "If there is a God who loves me, show me!"

Streak! A second star burst through the heavens as if proclaiming the sure promise of a loving God reaching out to a lost, confused soul. "Wow! What does this mean?" I exclaimed. My heart pounded madly against my ribs. This was too good to be true! Could it really be a sign from a loving God? Could it really mean there was a God who really, truly loved me?

My thoughts were beginning to polarize. My empty heart was feeling some semblance of faith. There was less fear and more hope. *I will try one more time, and that will be my answer.* I lifted my eyes toward the loving God and Father I did not know. I clenched my fists and for the third time prayed, "If there is a God who loves me, show me!"

Zoom! A stunning meteorite exploded through the great sea of stars with impressive clarity, declaring the wonderful, enduring, faithful love of the supreme God. "Oh!" was all I could utter. Time stood still as I sat on the cold, hard steps of that low, rambling barn. New hope surged through me as I suddenly realized there was indeed a God who loved me.

I sat there for a long, long time, my mind replaying the events of the last five years. I wished life could be the way it had been a few years ago. As long as I could remember, my dad and mom, Clarence and Ada, had argued a lot, but in spite of that, I loved them, and everything was as normal as in any other Amish home. Mom, the social one of my aging parents, was slender, gray-haired, not very tall, and wore glasses. She always had a smile for me when I came home.

Then there was Dad, short and stocky with round wire-rimmed glasses. Why did he have to get so angry when things didn't go the way he planned? I thought of the many times I had been blamed for something I hadn't done or thoroughly scolded for something I'd done wrong. Sometimes I wished Dad would just spank me instead of heaping upon me all the wrongs I had ever done. But though Dad had many faults, I could not help but feel sorry for him. Dad had a hearing problem, which made it hard for him to converse with others. His hearing impairment had kept him from learning well in school. His reading comprehension and writing skills were only about a third-grade level.

At home, Dad would read a German prayer every morning in a barely audible voice. We read the Scriptures only every other Sunday, though Dad almost never helped because he couldn't read well or understand what was read. Neither did he receive much spiritual food from the church services because of not being able to hear the minister.

Our Amish church had services only every two weeks. Some members used the off Sundays to visit other congregations. Others stayed home and rested or used the day as they pleased. My family usually stayed home on these in-between Sundays.

As I looked up into the now-peaceful sky, my thoughts returned to my mother. She had found it difficult to give up her traditional values and lose contact with her parents and siblings, but she had believed we were doing the right thing and had been willing to make whatever sacrifices she must. Now my heart ached for her. I thought of the times when I had been disobedient and wished I could tell her I was sorry. But right now things were too tangled to apologize. Apologizing would be expressing doubt. "No, I can't let anyone know how I feel," I said to myself. "Never!"

Chapter 2

A Thirst for More

Five years earlier, in the spring of 1988, Mom had announced at the supper table, "There will be a meeting tomorrow night at Jason Yoder's place." Suppertime usually served as the communication link for our large Old Order Amish family. There were twelve children in all, though only five of us still lived at home. We sat around the table by age.

Dark-haired Carolyn, the oldest of us five, sat at the end of the kitchen table. Her friendly personality and ready laugh made it easy to overlook her slight stutter. David was next in line. He was also dark-haired and easygoing. He had been going steady with Mary Wengerd for a while already. Calvin sat beside David. He had light, sandy hair and was more quiet and reserved. Toby, tall and red-haired, sat between Calvin and me. He had just turned sixteen. I was fourteen.

I leaned forward. "What is the meeting about?"

"A speaker from Romania will give a talk about his experiences under communism," answered my mother.

"That sounds interesting. Do we all get to go?" wondered Toby.

Mom looked at Dad, but he had not heard the conversation. "Huh?" he asked, raising his eyebrows inquiringly. Mom explained what had been said.

"I don't know why not. It's just five miles over to Jason's," responded Dad in his easygoing manner. He was generally a man of few words.

"Oh, good," I replied. "That sounds like fun!"

The next evening our ten thousand broilers were fed in record time. Everybody worked like a team. "I wish we could work together like this all the time," I said, my head in the feed bin.

"So do I," replied Toby. "Even Mom and Dad seem happier tonight."

"I noticed that too. I feel more secure when they're getting along."

"Same here," responded Toby, scooping another ration of feed into the chicken feeder. "I enjoy it if everyone can be relaxed and at ease."

We finished our chores in companionable silence.

Everyone was ready to go by 5:30. We piled into two buggies, and soon the horses' steady clips ate up the five miles.

"It looks like we're early," remarked Toby. "There are only five other buggies here."

"I see that," I answered. "It feels good for a change. It's embarrassing to always be the last to arrive."

I followed the rest of the family toward the building. "That must be his car," I observed, noticing a little blue Ford close to the entrance. "Apparently he's not living in Indiana, because it has an out-of-state license plate," I remarked.

An hour later I sat spellbound, listening with an eagerness that was unusual for me. Usually during church services I spent my time whispering with a friend or cleaning my fingernails with my pocketknife, but not tonight. Listening to a speech by a real persecuted Romanian was quite different from the predictable sermons I was used to. I listened intently as an interpreter translated the speech line by line.

"After beating me for twenty minutes, the guard dragged me back into my cold, damp cell," cried Demitrial Dudimar. "I couldn't walk, couldn't talk, couldn't even sit up by myself. The bed of straw with a dirty sheet crumpled on top felt like heaven after receiving three of those beatings in one day.

"After lying on the bed for ten minutes, barely conscious, I heard the heavy footsteps of a guard marching down the concrete hall. 'Now what,' I wondered. 'Will I be dragged out again and beaten to death this time?' "

I shivered. *It would be awful to be tormented like that, and for no reason. Why, he was a good man! Why would they treat a man like a criminal just because he loved Jesus? I wonder if I love Jesus like that. I'm sure I couldn't have stood those beatings.* My thoughts tumbled on.

Demitrial continued. "Then I heard a key screeching in the old rusty lock on my steel door. The bolt made a grinding sound as it unlocked, and the door swung open."

The atmosphere felt charged as we all waited in suspense.

" 'Demitrial! Demitrial!' The tone of voice was urgent, yet soft. I opened my eyes only because I was so surprised at the tone." Beads of perspiration stood on Demitrial's forehead like so many drops of dew. "I was not prepared for what I saw. I expected the usual gray uniform and tall black boots, but this guard was dressed in a pure white robe!" Demitrial swung his arms high.

" 'I am Gabriel, your guardian angel!' the man in white declared. 'Stand up! Come with me!' His tone was urgent. 'You have a great mission to accomplish, and I must show you what it is.'

"Suddenly I felt myself being gently lifted off the uncomfortable mattress. My pain was gone!" Demitrial gestured with his hands.

I listened, spellbound. *That sounds like a miracle,* I thought. *It would really be something to see an angel.* A deep desire was stirring in the depths of my soul—a yearning for something more meaningful, more spiritually satisfying than what I had now.

"I was suddenly lifted high above the prison, right through the roof," continued Demitrial. "Gabriel held me underneath his body as we flew swiftly and silently over the earth. The earth became smaller and smaller, as if I were in a great rocket speeding into space."

Demitrial paused for a sip of water while his interpreter wiped his forehead with a white handkerchief. This was getting the crowd's attention. His listeners sat erect and suspense filled the air.

I was thinking rapidly. *How can this be? A ride with an*

angel? He must have a tremendous connection with God. It must be awesome to have such a vision, or whatever that was. I remembered Dad telling a story of a man who supposedly had a vision, but nothing like this. *Demitrial must be a real man of God,* I concluded. *Maybe sort of like John the Baptist.*

Suddenly Demitrial thrust his long arms into the air. "Rise!" he commanded. We hesitated a bit until someone in the front row stood up, and slowly everybody followed suit. "Hallelujah!" Demitrial shouted charismatically. He was obviously unfamiliar with the Amish hesitancy to openly express emotions, especially in public. He looked a bit bewildered when no one responded. "Hallelujah!" he cried the second time.

Slowly the crowd responded with a subdued, "Hallelujah!"

Pleased at this response, Demitrial pumped his arms two or three times. "Amen!" he concluded his little emotional exercise.

"Amen!" the crowd repeated obediently.

Well, I wonder how that will go over, I thought, half amused. *That was kind of neat.* A tingling sensation was still traveling down my spine as I settled down for the rest of the story.

"We were flying through a great black space; then suddenly we broke through and I saw a large city with many, many tall buildings and skyscrapers," continued the refreshed Demitrial. "We passed over another great city, and another one, and then Gabriel spoke." Demitrial's voice was high-pitched and animated by now. He grabbed a small hand towel and mopped his forehead. "And Gabriel spoke to me," he repeated with a triumphant tone and a happy gleam in his eyes.

Wow, he must be a real prophet, I pondered, and briefly wondered what a prophet actually was. I remembered the preachers telling stories about the prophet Elijah from the Bible. If I remembered right, Elijah prayed, and God sent fire down from heaven, and the fire was so hot it burned everything on the altar and the altar itself.

Demitrial did not wait for my thoughts to return to his story. "Gabriel said that these great cities are in America, and they are full of wickedness," he continued. "America is a very prosperous nation, but it is also full of violence and ungodliness. The Father will punish America for this!" he shouted. The interpreter looked too timid to repeat the words with the same volume Demitrial spoke them. "These cities," gestured the keyed-up Demitrial, "were in New York, Florida, and California." He paused to let this penetrate. "Before the year 2000 God will totally destroy these three states," he prophesied.

My mouth dropped open at this news. I heard several other people gasp. *Totally destroy? I wonder how that will come about.* I shuddered involuntarily. *At least none of them are very close to us,* I comforted myself. I thought of our rural Lagrange County, Indiana, farmstead and could not help wondering what would become of it if it were in New York rather than here. *Such a powerful connection.* I wondered again at this Romanian's vision.

I didn't hear much of the rest of Demitrial's speech. *Those cities will be destroyed,* I repeated over and over in my mind. *I wonder how the destruction will take place.* I could not help but feel a bit worried about the prophecy. *I wonder what Dad thinks about this man,* I thought.

I shivered as I thought about the destruction that was to occur in America. *Why does America have to be so wicked?* I wondered. *Why doesn't everybody believe in God? I guess I am fortunate to know about God and Jesus. Not everybody has the privilege of being Amish like we are and having the real faith.* I felt a bit uneasy as I thought about this. I knew I longed to live like our English neighbors and sow my wild oats when I turned sixteen. Many of the Amish youth dressed like the rest of society, drove automobiles, smoked cigarettes, and partied after they turned sixteen. *I wonder how that became accepted by the Amish,* I thought. *But at least most of them come back to the faith and make peace with God and the church.*

Actually, the Amish might not be so different from the rest of the world. My thoughts rambled on. *Didn't Demitrial say the churches in America are much the same as the churches in Romania were before persecution hit their country?* My thoughts went to the last church service at neighbor John's house. I couldn't forget the scene of the four young married men behind the barn smoking and telling dirty jokes after church. Why would they do that after hearing the sermon just an hour before? In fact, the minister said that smoking belongs to the world. *Why are they acting like that if they have made peace with God and the church?* I wondered. *Does driving a horse and buggy make peace with God? If it does, then I must be in pretty good shape. But somehow it doesn't seem like quite enough,* I concluded unhappily.

Later that night my thoughts continued marching after I had lain in bed for an hour without sleeping. *Is it really important to make peace with God? Who is God, anyway? Mom and Dad never seem to be able to really tell me. They just say He is up in heaven and He knows everything about everyone, and that we are Amish because our forefathers were Anabaptists and they suffered and some died for living that way.* My thoughts tumbled on. *That sounds like the Christians in Romania that Demitrial spoke about tonight.*

Dad seemed to think Demitrial was a real prophet of God. I recalled my father speaking favorably about him before he went to bed. He even said something about being glad the church could hear him tonight because it would be good to consider his warnings.

I yawned, looked at the clock, and gasped. *12:30 already! I have to get some sleep. We have to clean out the one chicken barn tomorrow. I can't figure it all out, anyway.* And with that, I rolled over, pulled the patchwork quilt up to my chin, and fell into a fitful sleep.

Chapter 3

Something New

Several weeks later, my family went to Floyd Miller's place for church services. They lived in a neighboring church district, and I was a bit nervous, since I didn't know many people there. I was relieved to see my married brother Manass as soon as I jumped down from the buggy.

"It's good to see you here!" I exclaimed as I heartily shook my brother's hand. Manass was five years older than I, several inches taller, and just as slender. "Will you be coming over to our house after church?" I inquired.

"Oh, I suppose we'll make it over in time for some popcorn and cider," Manass chuckled. "I wanted to talk to Dad about some things, anyway," he added mysteriously. The men were making their way into the house for the usual three-hour church service. Manass fell in line with the others close to his age.

I sauntered over to a group of boys huddled outside the barn. Suddenly they tilted their heads back and laughed hysterically. *What are they laughing about?* I asked myself. Then I saw my friend Ben lift both arms and whoop, "Hallelujah, amen!" The boys burst out laughing, some of them holding their sides. I felt a sudden dread. *They must be talking about Demitrial's meeting the other evening,* I surmised. I turned and stalked away, my face coloring with anger. "The nerve," I muttered disgustedly.

It was 2:30 when I finally opened the door into our own kitchen after unhitching Prince, the faithful buggy horse Toby and I drove. I stepped into the house and noticed a hat and a bonnet on the kitchen table. *Manass and Wilma must be here already,* I guessed. I stopped at the wash sink and filled a glass with cold water. *Mmm, this tastes so good on a warm day like this,* I mused contentedly. Low voices coming from the living room confirmed my suspicions that the visitors were already here. *I'll run up to my room and change my clothes,* I decided, quickening my steps after I spotted the popcorn popper.

I kicked off my shoes and headed for the stairs. My right foot was on the fourth step when Manass's voice brought me up short. My mouth dropped and my chest tightened as I listened to the conversation floating up the staircase.

"How did you like Demitrial's meeting? It was even better than I expected!" Manass exclaimed before Dad could answer.

"He really had some warnings for us," Dad agreed. "Did I hear someone say you were involved in setting up the meeting?"

"That's right," Manass agreed. "One of my coworkers heard him speak in South Bend. He said we must arrange for him to speak to the Amish. He gave me Demitrial's telephone number and I called him. He agreed to come right away."

I leaned hard against the wall. *So that's how he showed up.*

"I believe the churches here are not serious enough about being spiritual," Manass went on.

I wonder what he means by that. It seemed strange to hear him using the word "spiritual."

The conversation drifted on. Suddenly Manass leaned forward in his chair.

"By the way, did you hear that rumor about the Amishman who has visions from God? He claims that Shipshewana is like Sodom and Gomorrah of the Bible."

"I-yi-yi," Dad responded soberly. "He may be right. There is so much money made by the Amish name. It has long been a burden to me that the churches do not all seem to be following what our forefathers taught us. I think we may be losing our spirituality, like Demitrial said the other evening. It is sobering to think about. I wonder what we can do about it. Sometimes I get an urge to search more for God, but I am not sure where to go."

"This Amishman I was talking about—Wilbur Lee Eash —he seems to have some answers," Manass suggested.

"Where does this Wilbur Lee Eash live?" inquired Dad.

"A little past US 5, over by Shipshewana," replied Manass. "I pass his place when I go to work."

I turned from the conversation and resumed my trip up the stairs. I quickly changed into my everyday clothes and returned to the living room to visit. The topic had switched to farming, gardening, and raising broilers. I forgot about the Wilbur Lee Eash conversation until later that day.

That evening at the supper table, after Manass and Wilma had left, Dad resumed the conversation about Wilbur Lee Eash. "Manass says he has visions from God. Wilma's parents, Melvin and Ellen Miller, seem to agree. Melvin and Ellen visited him after his wife died of cancer, and he talked a lot about his connection with God. Manass says he and Wilma are interested in visiting him to see firsthand what it's all about. Mom and I might go too if they bring back a good report."

"That sounds a bit like Demitrial, doesn't it?" I queried. "It seems like he has a strong connection with God or something."

"Well, it would kind of sound like it," replied Dad. "But we'll see what Manass says after they visit him. They are planning to go next Tuesday evening."

"I really wonder what they will find out," I said. "For some reason I hope it goes well. I wouldn't mind meeting the man myself."

I could not understand my feelings about this strange turn of events. First, this Demitrial was impacting the community with his visions and stories of persecution. Now here was another man seeing visions apparently from God. I had never thought so deeply about life before. Outside of occasionally questioning my Amish lifestyle and Anabaptist heritage, I was mostly content to live as my parents instructed. Spiritual conversations were not common in our home. We saved our study of Scripture and talk of the Bible for our three-hour church service.

Why don't we study the Bible more? I pondered many questions as I lay on my bed that night. *Why don't the ministers in our church encourage more Bible reading? Is it true that it will make us proud or maybe make us join worldly churches? Are all churches that drive cars worldly? Is it worldlier to drive a car than to ride in one? What do the ministers mean when they say that you might become worldlier by reading the Bible too much? There must be some spirituality here, because we share a close, simple lifestyle, go to church every two weeks, and the members have Communion twice a year.*

I remembered someone remarking that good farmers don't have devotions. *Are daily devotions worldly? Is farming a spiritual experience?* I wondered wearily. I wondered how it would be to have devotions every day. *Alva and Elnora have devotions. They are Amish and they don't farm. Is that why they need to have devotions? They must know something about God too,* I thought. *I wonder what Alva would say about Wilbur Lee?*

My brother Alva had married and moved away from the large settlement in Indiana and joined a small Amish community in Mio, Michigan, where they encouraged families to spend time in daily prayer and Bible reading.

My family doesn't seem very spiritual, I thought sadly, recalling my parents' angry conversations. *Why can't they be more* geduldig *(patient) with each other?* I felt my chest tighten. It made me feel protected when they lived peaceably rather than in tension.

I wonder if Wilbur Lee has spiritual answers like Demitrial does, I thought hopefully. *Maybe he could help our family live more happily together.* A twinge of excitement passed through me.

Suddenly the inconsistencies I observed in my Amish community repulsed me. *If they want to be Amish just because their forefathers were, then they can. I want to be spiritual like Demitrial and Wilbur Lee.* I felt a twinge of anger. *There has to be more to this life than driving a horse and buggy, doing without electricity, and using outhouses!* I thought daringly. *I hope Mom and Dad will go visit Wilbur Lee soon— real soon.*

The following Wednesday evening, Manass appeared at the door.

"Come in! Come in!" exclaimed Mom, happy to see her son. She held the door for Manass and Wilma. "We are glad to see you tonight!" She paused for a moment and looked admiringly into her tall son's eyes. A knowing look passed between them. "Just bring your wraps into the kitchen and lay them on the table," she continued.

Dad slowly rose from his chair. "Come into the living room where it's more comfortable to visit," he suggested. I followed the others into the living room, hoping to hear about Manass's visit with Wilbur Lee.

"Well, did you get to visit with Wilbur Lee?" Mom asked even before she was seated. Somehow, Wilbur Lee had found residence in our hearts before we even knew him.

Manass cleared his throat. "Yes, we did," he began seriously, stroking his auburn hair. "We spent two hours there last night, and it seemed like ten minutes. This man has something we don't have, and I would trade the world to find it," he stated with emotion.

Mom moved to the edge of her chair. "What did you talk about?"

"Well, for one thing, we didn't talk about the price of feeder pigs, my job at the trailer factory, or anything remotely close. What we talked about was spiritual. It was about the Bible. This man knows his Bible if anyone does. He has a real connection with the Father—the heavenly Father, that is. He calls him Father. And you can see he thinks of Him as a real father. It was just real touching."

My heart thumped. *Sounds like he hit pay dirt.* I wondered fleetingly what this man's ministers thought about him. *Do they think he's spiritual too? Will he be driving a car soon?* My thoughts tumbled around in my head.

"Dad, did you know that it takes more than just being Amish to be saved?" Manass continued, interrupting my thoughts. "Being a member of the Amish church or living and dressing like our ancestors is not enough to get us to heaven. Wilbur Lee says the Father is not pleased with our good works if our hearts are not connected with Him."

Dad leaned forward, obviously interested. "You mean this is what Wilbur Lee and you were talking about? Is this what he believes? Did he find this in the Bible?"

"Yes, and more than just that. The devil is out there to deceive us. He has tremendous power, but if we have the Father's Spirit within us, we can rebuke him and he will leave us. Satan tormented Wilbur Lee's wife with so much pain when she had cancer that she could hardly bear it. Wilbur Lee had to rebuke Satan in the Father's name repeatedly to give her the comfort she needed."

"It sounds like he has a real connection with God like Demitrial does," remarked Mom, who had been listening intently.

"Yes, I would say he definitely does."

"Did he show any *hochmut* (pride) when he spoke?" asked Dad.

"No, and that is why I was so impressed with him. He was very friendly and just showed a genuine interest in our spiritual life. He says we are saved by faith in God, through His grace, and not by any works we have done. He says the ministers don't quite agree with him, but this is how he understands the Bible according to the revelations of the Father's Spirit. He says we can know that we are saved through Jesus if we have a connection with the Father and do as He commands."

"I wonder what his ministers would say if they knew he was talking to people like you," I questioned.

"Well, it sounds like they had several conversations that didn't go too well, so the Spirit revealed that he should not talk to them about these things anymore. His love for the Father is so great that he will not let any man come between them. He would do anything except disobey the Father." Manass looked soberly at his listeners. "This man is serious about his faith. As I said, we did not waste any time talking about carnal things like pigs or the horse sale. Even though we hear a lot being preached about our Anabaptist forefathers, he seems to be living and believing more like them than what we are used to here."

"Uh-huh," grunted Dad.

"What's more, he says that few people listen to him when he wants to talk about the spiritual condition of the church. In fact, some people actually purposely turn their backs when he passes them in the marketplace. He gets the feeling they think he is weird. However, he is determined to love them even if the persecution hurts. He says the rejection reminds him of how he was mocked as a boy growing up. He spoke quite a while about his school days.

He did not have any friends, and his schoolmates threw rocks at him and called him terrible names. I guess it had to do with his family or something."

"I-yi-yi," clucked Dad sadly, shaking his head, a faraway look in his eyes. "I need to visit him."

I knew Dad had had some unpleasant experiences while growing up. His speech and hearing impediments may have triggered some of the mockery he endured. I recalled some of the stories Dad told of being made fun of at school. My fists clenched instinctively and my face was set with anger.

Why does that wicked stuff have to happen? My thoughts exploded. *This is a terrible, evil world. Why do people hate each other?* I couldn't remember ever being mocked. I was the leader among my friends. They seemed to like my funny ways and easy laugh. The last thing I wanted was to be mocked like my father.

Dad spoke again. "Manass, do you think he would welcome us if we came over for the evening?"

"Oh, I'm sure he would be glad to speak with more concerned church people. The spiritual condition of our people weighs on him," replied Manass. "I would certainly give it a try."

Chapter 4

First Impressions

"Oh, really!" I responded in surprise. Mom had just informed the family that we were going to visit Wilbur Lee the next evening after supper. My heart beat faster. My parents' new interest in spiritual things made me feel warm inside and gave me a sense of security. "That sounds interesting. Who all is going?"

The next evening found Dad, Mom, and the five of us children who still lived at home on Wilbur Lee's doorstep. I shivered slightly as I heard heavy footsteps approaching the door in response to Dad's knock.

A short, heavyset, middle-aged man opened the door. *"Kumet on nei!"* (Come on in!) he invited pleasantly. A smile lit his bearded face. Although he was only thirty-eight, he was already balding, making him look a bit older. Wilbur Lee warmly shook hands with each of us.

After the initial formalities, Mom spoke. "We were so sorry to hear that Maribeth passed away and how much she had to suffer."

"Yes, it was very hard to see her suffer for so long." Wilbur Lee's voice quivered with emotion. "The Father and I were drawn closer together through this experience. I was thankful for the treatment we found to help ease her suffering."

"What kind of treatment did the doctors use?" Dad asked.

"They started with radiation and chemotherapy," Wilbur Lee explained. "After many treatments, the tests showed little improvement. The doctor admitted he had little experience with that form of treatment. He essentially sent her home to die."

"I-yi-yi," Dad sympathized. "It seems the doctors don't know as much as they let on."

"After we came home, I began searching for other treatments. I prayed desperately to the Father for answers."

"Did you try natural methods?" Dad asked.

"Yes. We went to an herb doctor," he answered. "He usually tested which herbs to use by placing the bottle on the patient's throat while he stretched out his arm. If the doctor could push the patient's arm down, the patient did not need that herb. If the arm remained strong, it was the correct herb. Maribeth was too weak to use this method, so he held the bottle against her throat and used the same test with his own fingers to get an answer."

"Did the herbs help?" Mom asked.

"Yes. She got steadily better and was soon well enough to attend church again. Our first doctor said that in itself was a miracle, as he had not expected her to get better at all."

"That is really something," Dad remarked.

"After a while I decided to try the finger testing method myself," Wilbur Lee continued. "I was surprised to find it actually worked! In fact, I found that I could even use it to find answers in other areas, even spiritually."

"That's very interesting!" Mom exclaimed. "It's too bad it didn't completely cure her."

"Yes, it was hard to understand," Wilbur Lee responded sadly. "I would have preferred that she be healed, but the Father willed it differently. It was painful to watch her suffer. We got a lot of visitors, but often they just did not understand what we were going through. Sometimes I did not allow visitors in the house because she was too low. Some people did not understand why we had to limit visitors, and they rejected us. In fact, it reminded me of the rejection I got when I was younger."

"Really?" Dad asked, leaning forward in his chair.

"When I was growing up, my schoolmates were not nice to me," Wilbur Lee continued. "They mocked me constantly in school. I did not have a nice home life, and it seemed everybody knew it. But why didn't the ministers try to help my parents? Why did everybody know about our situation, yet nothing changed?" His voice sounded bitter.

"Is that right?" sympathized Dad. "I know how that feels."

For the next thirty minutes Dad shared from his heart the painful experiences of his youth. The conversation was uninterrupted except for an occasional empathetic clucking from Wilbur Lee, spurring Dad from one painful experience to the next.

Finally, Mom mentioned the time. Much to our

surprise, it was nearly ten o'clock.

"We really must be going," agreed Dad. "The time went by fast."

"I am glad you came. We don't feel like strangers anymore after only one visit," said Wilbur Lee. "Goodnight." He smiled and shook our hands again as we walked out into the dark night.

* * *

On Saturday morning a little over a week later, Manass stepped into the house, announcing his arrival with a hearty, "Hello!"

"Oh, hello! Come in!" Mom welcomed him.

After some small talk, Manass started in. "Did you hear that Melvin and Ellen are visiting Wilbur Lee every week?" he asked, referring to his in-laws.

"Why are they seeing him that often?" I asked.

"On their second visit he really shared his revelations from the Spirit. He is definitely a Spirit-filled person. After our second visit with him we found the same thing. He teaches from the Bible and has given us some real answers already," he said excitedly. "I think you should visit him again."

"He did seem close to God," Mom agreed. "Would he tell us more if we visited him again?"

"I certainly think he would," Manass encouraged. He stood up to leave.

"I think we should see him again," Calvin spoke up. "I would like to know what he has to say."

"Same here," I agreed. A strange desire stirred in me— a desire for something more meaningful.

40

Several days later found us on Wilbur Lee's doorstep once again.

"Come in!" he welcomed us eagerly.

We sat in his living room, and the conversation naturally drifted to Maribeth's illness.

Wilbur Lee's voice was soft and trembled just slightly. "It was a very difficult time—a bitter battle with the devil, the arch enemy of the Father. The Father and I have total victory over the devil and his curses. We must be more aware of his presence and his subtle ways of attack. All illness and pain come from the enemy, but we don't need to be subject to it!"

Wow, this must be real to him! And the way he refers to God as "the Father" sounds so personal and spiritual! I noted.

"Yes," continued Wilbur Lee, "Maribeth suffered a tremendous amount of pain with her cancer. She would moan and cry out in pain toward the end of her life. At times I just begged in intercession with the Father to relieve her."

"I-yi-yi," clucked Mom sympathetically.

"That must have been very hard," Dad agreed. "Did the Father hear you?" he asked rather awkwardly, not being used to such terms.

Wilbur Lee leaned back in his chair, his eyes rolled slightly upward, gazing at the ceiling. "Did He ever!" he exclaimed softly. "Oh, the Father and I, we have such a blessed connection!" For a moment he seemed lost in time, oblivious of his curious visitors.

I shivered in spite of myself. It seemed a bit strange to me, but I didn't quite know what to expect from one who had such a connection with the Father.

"You know," continued our host, "I wish all the Amish people could have the Spirit of the Father without measure, but the Father gives of His Spirit in measure to those of His children He chooses. His prophets, especially, were filled with a great measure of His Spirit. He worked great and mighty works through them. He counseled and directed His people through them. We must be such that the Father can do His work through us. That is why we must obey the Father and have this spiritual connection with Him."

None of us spoke, and after a short silence, Wilbur Lee continued. "One evening stands out to me in particular. We had visitors after supper." He paused to wet his lips. "After the visitors left, Maribeth was in such agonizing pain that she could hardly bear it. I pleaded with the Father for help. Suddenly, I felt this great dark cloud pressing over me, nearly suffocating me. I knew it was Satan's presence, and I knew he was the one responsible for her pain, for it is not the Father's will that any of his children should suffer so. In desperation, I rebuked him. 'In Jesus' name, depart!' Immediately the cloud disappeared and Maribeth's pain left her. I was so blessed and humbled that the Father cared. His Son Jesus is very real to me. I just wish He could be more real to my brothers and sisters in the church," he concluded, repeating his spiritual longing.

"And!" he added emphatically, leaning forward in his rocker, "I believe the curses came from some of the visitors. The Spirit revealed this more than once to me." His voice trembled slightly. "When one is out of harmony with the Father, he can cast a spell on those about him. For example, one of the churchwomen went into the bedroom to see Maribeth. She was in there a full hour before coming out.

Maribeth was terribly upset when I went in to check on her. I just knew in my heart that woman was the cause of her pain."

Silence fell over the group. Nobody dared break it. These were new thoughts for us. His insights were deeply unsettling, yet they seemed based on the truth. Spiritual conversation seemed second nature for him, especially compared to what we were used to in church. We felt drawn together in our spirits.

Dad finally broke the silence. "This is really something, Wilbur Lee. We are interested in learning more about spiritual things. You have a way of explaining these things so that they make sense and we can understand them."

"Mm-hm," agreed Mom. The spiritual hunger was evident in my family's hearts. "You need to speak with the ministers about these things," Mom added.

"Oh, no!" exclaimed Wilbur Lee. "They would never listen to me. They are not open to the Father's words. They understand the Bible only according to traditional interpretation. They believe we are saved through the good works we do. That is not what the Bible actually teaches. The Father teaches us that we are saved through grace. It was because His Son Jesus, who was His greatest prophet, died on the cross. His blood made atonement for our sins. The priests do not need to offer up animals as they did in the Old Testament to appease the Father's anger. It is because of the Father's love and Jesus' death and resurrection, not by our good works, that we are saved.

"Think about it." He lowered his voice. "How can a minister attend an auction all day Saturday, still do the milking, and have time left to study for his sermon the next morning? They just preach from memory."

"That makes sense," agreed Dad.

"I spend hours on my knees praying and seeking answers from God," he continued soberly. "We have to be serious about this Christian life."

He must be really sincere, I thought admiringly.

"A lot of Amish just read a prayer out of a prayer book, go their way, and never seek an answer from God." He was looking at Dad. "We can truly get answers directly from God."

Dad looked uncomfortable. I remembered his mumbled prayer this morning. It certainly fit Wilbur Lee's description.

"These are all new teachings for us," Dad said as he looked at the clock. "We should be heading home."

"I can see that you are spiritually hungry and looking for answers," Wilbur Lee said feelingly. "I didn't think you would come back after the first visit. I thought you might be more interested in the material things of this world, but I see that you are not."

"My Mom taught me not to love material things and was a very spiritually-minded person. She accepted me the way I was. I can feel the same connection with you that I had with her," Dad shared. "We'd like to hear more of your experiences."

"If you want to learn more about spiritual matters, you are more than welcome to come over any time," he invited graciously. "I knew before you came in this evening that you would receive what I had to share," he added mystically.

"Goodnight," he said with feeling as we got up to leave.

"Goodnight," our family responded as we stepped out into the starless night. The wind was starting to whip and raindrops began to fall as we hurried to our two buggies.

Thunder rumbled in the distance as the horse trotted home late that Thursday night. The thunderclap sounded ominously like a book closing—one book closing to the opening of another. Was it a sign?

OUT OF DECEPTION

Chapter 5

The New Leader

The rattle of buggy wheels alerted our family that someone was driving in the lane. Mom glanced out. "Oh, it's Manass and Wilma." She slipped off her covering and went to get a more presentable one. When she came back, she looked at the clock and sighed. "Why is Dad not in yet?"

I had finished my chores and was reading a book. "He was going to check on the pigs yet when I came in," I answered.

My brothers and I had finished the other chores, and the family had been waiting on Dad twenty minutes now. We often had to wait on him. It was 7:45, and we had not eaten supper yet.

"Come on in," we heard Mom say as the outside door opened.

Manass and his young wife walked into the kitchen. Wilma walked with a noticeable limp. I remembered the shocking accident that had caused her limp. One evening when she was walking home from work, a car had hit her from behind, throwing her violently forward and breaking her back. Everyone was amazed how she had miraculously pulled through, even when the doctors had not given her much hope. I admired how Manass had stayed faithful to her even though they had not been married yet.

"Oh, you haven't eaten yet?" Wilma asked, seeing the table set for supper.

"No," Mom replied simply. "Dad is not in yet, but I hear him coming now."

"So, how was your evening with Wilbur Lee?" Manass inquired eagerly as everyone gathered around the supper table.

"We had a wonderful evening!" Mom replied enthusiastically.

Manass smiled in spite of himself. He could see that his parents had a hold on something big—very big. "I'm not surprised you feel that way," he continued. "That is how we found him; in fact, how everybody finds him who is fortunate to be welcomed by him."

"What do you mean by that?" I asked.

"Well, he doesn't talk about these things to just everybody who comes to visit, like the ministers for example. They oppose his teachings, and they tell him he should not talk to others about the things of the Father."

"Why not?" I asked, a little puzzled.

"I guess they are afraid he will draw people away from the church and create a split. But if they are feeding their members enough spiritual food, they should not have to worry about that. I just wish they would listen to him. They might learn a few Bible truths themselves."

"But how does he know who to welcome and start teaching these things?" I remembered the remark Wilbur Lee had made about knowing our family would receive his teachings before we walked in the door.

Manass seemed to know what I was thinking. "He has such a strong connection with the Father that he knows some things in advance," he explained. "He can tell before people enter his front door if they will listen to him or if they are only there to challenge his teachings and his spiritual experiences."

"But how can he tell?" My curiosity was piqued. This was getting deeper than I had anticipated. *I'm sure glad he accepted us,* I thought with relief. The food on my plate was momentarily forgotten.

"It seems rather simple," admitted Manass. "He says that one time when Maribeth was so sick, they took her to this alternative medical practitioner who could check medication and even make a diagnosis by asking yes and no questions. When he asked a question such as, "Is this the correct herb or medicine?" he pressed down on his middle finger with his index finger. If he had the strength to push the middle finger down, he had a "no" answer. If his middle finger remained strong, then it was a "yes" answer.

"Yes, he mentioned that," Mom responded.

"Oh, did he? Anyway, Wilbur Lee tried it at home for Maribeth's medication, and it worked. He then started asking other types of questions, especially spiritual ones, and he got the same results. The Father definitely connects with him this way, and Wilbur Lee can tell you many experiences he has had. This is how he knows whether people will listen to him before they enter his house."

"I see," I said slowly, still trying to understand this system.

"I guess if it works, it must be from God, or the Father, as Wilbur Lee says," Mom noted. Dad said nothing.

The room was silent for a while. Then Manass cleared his throat, breaking the silence. "I'm sure he knows the Father's will about his way of seeking answers, even if it seems a little strange to us now. We will probably understand it better the more we get to know him. He definitely uses it for the good of others. I guess that's the main thing."

"When are you planning to visit him again?" asked Mom as she started clearing the table.

"I don't know," replied Manass. "We think we should be careful how often we go over there. He always welcomes us, but we don't want to arouse unnecessary suspicions. It is encouraging to hear of others going to see him. They usually have inspiring bits of conversation to relate."

"Are Melvin and Ellen Miller still seeing him regularly?" asked Dad.

"Yes, they are still going every week. I am a little concerned about their standing with the ministers. I overheard their deacon and one of the preachers talking quite seriously at the sale barn last week. They sounded like they were going to tell them to quit seeing Wilbur Lee. I am not sure how Melvin will respond, because his confidence in the ministers is pretty well shot. I just feel things tightening up around here."

"Has anyone else in your church showed any interest

or opposition?" asked Mom.

"No, but people do seem a little more quiet. I see more and more people huddled together, two or three in a group, talking in undertones. It makes me uncomfortable. I can still visit with a few of my friends about our work in the trailer factories or about the latest hog and horse prices. If I try to talk about some of the biblical teachings I've learned from Wilbur Lee, such as connecting with the Father's Spirit or being saved from our sins through the grace of God, they just shut down and look confused and sometimes even frightened."

"Well, well, that's too bad. I don't think it's right that people around here aren't more open to these things," Mom sympathized.

"One of my friends and I were talking about how so many of our young folks sow their wild oats when they come to the *rumschpringa* age. I mentioned that they really need the Father and to have their sins forgiven by the blood of Jesus. He said he's not quite sure what I mean, but he is sure that if they would just be willing to be baptized, submit themselves to the *ordnung* of the church, and do all the good they can, he is sure they would have a good chance of being saved in the end.

"I told him that doing all the good we can is not enough to satisfy the Father, but we have to depend totally on the grace of God and do what He tells us through His prophets in the Bible, and then we can be saved. He said that isn't what we have been taught by our forefathers, and if we can't do enough good works, then God's grace makes up for the rest.

"I could tell he wasn't really interested in believing that

God's grace alone has the power to save him. Of course, I believe that we must also do the Father's will. Through the Bible, His prophets gave us many instructions over the years. Jesus is the Father's greatest prophet, so we must follow His commands and teachings."

"Yes, I believe you are right," said Dad. "Wilbur Lee certainly understands the Bible well. We should take his teachings seriously. I think we should see him again soon. He really listened to the many painful experiences I had while growing up. He has an understanding way about him."

"What does Peter say?" Mom asked, referring to my oldest brother.

"Peter and Sadie are opposed to him," said Manass with a heavy look. "I just told them that they really couldn't make a true judgment until they personally visited Wilbur Lee and listened with open hearts. After two hours of persuasion, they finally committed themselves to go."

"Oh, I'm so glad to hear that they are going!" Mom exclaimed. "Sadie has been such a blessing to the family already. She has such a caring way about her and has helped us be more organized here in the house. If she would believe him, then Peter would too. That would make me so happy!"

Manass smiled at his mother. "Yes, she has brought stability to our family already. She seems to have spiritual depth."

That night I went to bed feeling satisfied that we were indeed on the right road. Anticipation filled me as I wondered what the future held.

Chapter 6

New Teachings

Over the next couple months we visited Wilbur Lee almost every week. We spent many hours discussing the Bible and hearing the latest revelations from the Spirit.

One night we were preparing for another visit. Calvin, Toby, and I hurried as fast as we could to get our chores done in time. Even so, it seemed that we always came in just a bit late. We ran for the house to wash up, grab a bite of supper, and change our clothes.

Supper was ready, but Mom and Dad were not in sight. Suddenly we heard loud, frustrated voices coming from the washhouse. We boys looked uneasily at each other and shrugged our shoulders. "Hard telling what happened," muttered Toby. The fighting was not unusual, but it turned my stomach into a hard knot.

Why all the arguing? I thought unhappily. *It doesn't seem to get them anywhere.* I looked at the clock. Six o'clock already! "We'd better hurry!" I exclaimed to my brothers.

"It's late!"

An hour and a half later, we finally arrived at Wilbur Lee's house. I had nearly forgotten about my parents' argument. I only wished we were earlier. We wouldn't have much time.

"Come on in!" Wilbur Lee beamed a friendly smile as he gave his familiar welcome. "How are you doing? It seems like a while since we visited." He gave each of us a hearty handshake. "Just take a seat wherever is comfortable. Here, take this rocker, Clarence."

I sat on the sofa beside my two brothers.

"So, have you experienced the joy of living closer to the Father?" Wilbur Lee asked unexpectedly, looking at Dad.

My heart thumped. *I wonder what made him ask that.* I remembered the conversation before supper. That hadn't sounded like the kind of talk the Father would approve of.

Dad's face appeared pained and he nervously cleared his throat. "Well," he finally ventured, "we really appreciate your teachings, and the many experiences you share are inspiring us to think more seriously about the Father."

"Good! I'm glad to hear that," beamed Wilbur Lee. "How do you feel, boys?" He looked straight at me.

I squirmed uncomfortably. *Why doesn't he start with Calvin? He's the oldest,* I thought. "I really enjoy our visits with you. They make me want to become more like the Father. I can tell you have a real connection with the Father's Spirit. I think everybody in the church would do well to listen to the Spirit's revelations through you. I just wish we wouldn't always be so late. That way we would have more time to visit with you." I blurted out the last bit without meaning to.

"Yes, the Spirit is faithful to reveal His will if we listen. The Bible says, 'He that has ears to hear, let him hear what the Spirit says unto the churches.' But sad to say, too many people just want to take their own selfish, carnal way," Wilbur Lee said, shaking his head sorrowfully. "We need the Spirit's direction. When we wake up in the morning, we need to ask Him to direct us in every little thing. So many people do not ask the Spirit for direction. If they want to go to town, they just go. If the wheel falls off, they just fix it and go on. All these things that happen are for a reason," he taught.

"How is your relationship with your family, Clarence?" he inquired kindly, abruptly changing the subject.

Dad was quiet for a long time, and then finally he admitted, "Mom and I do argue quite a bit, and I wish we could get help to overcome that."

Wilbur Lee nodded soberly. "I am pleased to hear you are open for help in this area. The enemy has control of you, and this must be broken. The Scriptures say we must be free from contention and strife. Where two people do not get along with each other, evil is present. This curse must be renounced.

"The same is true for you always being late," he counseled further. "This curse must be broken also."

"How do we get rid of these curses?" wondered Dad, a worried look on his face. "We don't want the enemy's curse over us!"

"Oh, no, you don't!" Wilbur Lee warned emphatically. "I'll tell you how. Say out loud, 'I rebuke you, Satan, in Jesus' name.' At times, you will hear a loud *snap!* Most people think this is just their house creaking. But actually, it is Satan's warning that he will be placing a curse upon you. Pray to the Father for help. He will help you with His Spirit."

* * *

Two weeks later Peter, Sadie, Manass, and Wilma came for a visit. The moment they entered the house, everyone could see they had something important to share. After everyone was comfortably seated in the living room, the conversation turned to Wilbur Lee. It was soon obvious that the tables had turned quite drastically after Peter and Sadie had visited him. They were impressed. Our family accepted the news heartily.

"Wilbur Lee taught us to look for seals," explained Peter. "This is something that happens to confirm that we are indeed following the truth. We must be Spirit led. If we get a leading from the Spirit and it comes to pass, then this is a seal. Wilbur Lee says it is important that we are sensitive to the Father's leading, whether through him or through the other group members. It is important that we support each other in this."

"Maybe we should get together every week at one of our homes," suggested Sadie. "That way one family at a time could visit Wilbur Lee and keep the suspicions down. That family could then relay his new teachings to the rest of us so we could all hear them. Wilbur Lee wouldn't even have to be at the meeting. I think we would all be more unified and strengthened, and we could share the seals we observe."

"That's a good idea!" I exclaimed. "We could all take turns."

"Sure; I like that idea," agreed Mom. "It would help keep the rumors down. Then whoever else might become interested could join our group. Monroe and Elsie showed some interest last week when they stopped in."

"I'll see if Melvin and Ellen and Wilbur Lee would be interested in this plan," volunteered Manass.

And so the group began. One family visited Wilbur Lee each week, and then anyone who was interested assembled at their house that Wednesday evening.

Soon the group grew to include most of Melvin's family and three of my married siblings, including my sister Elsie and her husband Monroe Miller. Altogether we had eight families. Often the evening stretched into the night as the host family shared Wilbur Lee's many experiences and teachings.

As time passed, we became increasingly convinced that Wilbur Lee had a real connection with God. He praised our faithfulness and spiritual eagerness. A close bond was forming between the families who joined in fellowship every Wednesday evening. We grew even closer as the suspicions and rumors from the surrounding communities escalated.

"Wilbur Lee told us something sobering last night," Manass announced one Wednesday evening when we had gathered at their house for another meeting.

He had everyone's attention immediately. I leaned forward in my chair.

Manass cleared his throat. "Wilbur Lee said we will suffer persecution for standing for the truth. We can expect that if we keep on meeting, the ministers will visit our homes soon and threaten to excommunicate us."

People gasped and darted nervous glances at one another.

"This sounds quite serious," Mom said.

"Yes, but what do they have to offer us?" Monroe asked.

"That's right. In fact, I heard Preacher Alvin yell at his children the other day. He must have been a quarter mile away!" someone else retorted.

That sure doesn't sound like love! I thought bitterly.

"One of the ministers in our church even smokes!" said another.

"We must stand firm in the truth. Wilbur Lee simply told us to listen to his revelations from the Father and we'll be safe," encouraged Manass. "In fact, he said the reason ministers sometimes preach with tears streaming down their cheeks is because they know they are ordained to deceive the people."

The room fell quiet.

Finally, Manass broke the stillness. "He wants us to keep this to ourselves. Do not talk to others about his teachings, especially not the ministers. We have something here. If we tell others, this could be taken away from us."

I felt more secure after hearing these inconsistencies exposed. *Wilbur Lee is our spiritual leader. He has the answers to our questions.*

We left that meeting more convinced than ever that Wilbur Lee had the truth.

* * *

Throughout the next several weeks, the ministers approached different members of the group and warned us of the direction we were taking. But we no longer trusted the ministers, and the nature of the issue made it difficult to communicate effectively. So the ministers' admonitions were interpreted as unloving attacks, and we began separating from our home congregations.

To complicate matters even more, Dad had a poor relationship with Deacon Dan Miller. One day Deacon Dan drove his buggy in the lane.

"Dan is coming, Dad," Mom said, sounding worried.

"Uh-oh," he grunted.

I watched Dan and Bishop Jake Bontrager climb down from the buggy. My heart skipped a beat. Why was Bishop Jake along? I was in the living room with Calvin and Toby. Mom, Dad, and Carolyn were in the kitchen. They spoke in low tones.

Knock, knock. The knocks made my heart jump.

Dad shuffled out to the entrance. "Come in," he greeted them.

The two ministers walked in, removing their broad-rimmed black hats. "Cold weather we're having," said Deacon Dan in an attempt at small talk.

Dad mumbled a response I couldn't understand.

Bishop Jake cleared his throat noisily. "We'd like to speak with you, Ada, and Carolyn privately," he stated, looking at Dad.

Wow, this doesn't sound good, I thought, shivering involuntarily.

Mom and Carolyn followed the three men out into the entryway and quietly pulled the door shut behind them. Twenty minutes later, the three came back into the kitchen and I saw the two ministers drive out the lane.

Dad looked pensive. Mom and Carolyn were quiet. Toby, Calvin, and I went out to the kitchen to find out what was going on.

"We have to either stop seeing Wilbur Lee or they will excommunicate us," Mom blurted out. She never could hide her feelings for long.

"That's just what I figured!" I responded angrily. "Why, he's just teaching us out of the Bible!"

"But we have to remember what all we learned from Wilbur Lee," Calvin reminded us. "He has helped our family tremendously already. This is more than the church was ever able to do. We must stand for what we know is the truth."

"I'd say you're right." Carolyn spoke for the first time.

"Isn't this exactly what Wilbur Lee predicted would happen just three weeks ago? I believe this is a seal from the Father," Toby suggested seriously.

A seal. I like that! The thought excited me. *We are working with the Spirit. This is heavy stuff.*

"I agree. This reminds me of when I was with the youth and I had to stand for what I knew was right. I was mocked for that." Dad spoke with feeling. "We are suffering persecution. We must do what we believe is right even if they don't understand us."

Chapter 7

Oaklawn

The next day Manass rode in the driveway at a gallop, his horse breathing hard. Dad, Mom, and I rushed out to meet him.

"The police came and arrested Wilbur Lee this morning!" he announced. "His dad and the doctor were with the police, and they had a court order to arrest him. His dad convinced the doctor that he was insane and violent just because of a grave the Father asked him to make in his garden. It was just a mound of earth. The Father told him to make it to break the curse that caused Maribeth's cancer."

"I-yi-yi," Dad clucked, worriedly shaking his head. "Where are the churches heading? Turning a man over to the police for something like that!"

"That is a good question. They put him in Oaklawn for now."

Oaklawn was a local mental institution. It was hardly a proper residence for a prophet.

Manass and my parents visited a bit longer, and Manass assured us he would keep us informed.

A few days later, Manass returned to give us an update.

"Wilbur Lee is in solitary confinement at the mental hospital. I visited him yesterday. He does not seem too discouraged. He believes he is being persecuted for his faith."

"What are they doing to him?" I inquired.

"They are trying to counsel him, but how can you counsel a prophet of God who is one with the Father?" Manass chuckled.

"I guess you are right," Mom agreed.

"Wilbur Lee told me he is simply not cooperating with them. For example, they put a bunch of pictures in front of him and asked him which one he would pick."

"Which one did he choose?" I asked, curious.

"He did not choose any."

"Why not?" I wondered.

"Because he knew that if he picked, say, a field of sunflowers, they would say he was lonely."

"Wilbur Lee is a wise man," Toby put in.

"Who will teach us now?" wondered Mom.

"Wilbur Lee told me to tell everybody that we must remain faithful to his teaching until he is released. He said that if we remain faithful to him, the Father's anointed, we will be saved from eternal destruction."

"Those are comforting words," replied Mom.

My heart beat faster to hear this clear promise. I

resolved in my heart to remain true to Wilbur Lee's teachings forever.

"Some of us are going to visit him tomorrow again. Would any of you want to go along?" Manass inquired.

"I want to go," I replied eagerly.

"So do I," came from all the others.

The next evening found a vanload of us on the way to Goshen. I sat right behind Manass. He turned and spoke to us. "I had an unusual experience yesterday."

My ears perked up.

"Remember how Wilbur Lee taught us to listen for Satan's warnings with snapping, cracking sounds in the house?"

"Certainly," I responded.

"Well, I kept hearing this snapping noise, and I simply knew this was Satan's presence. So I rebuked him in Jesus' name. The noise continued. I rebuked him repeatedly. Finally, I was getting desperate. Suddenly I had an idea, and it worked! The noises stopped immediately."

"What did you do?" Toby asked.

"I rebuked Satan in Wilbur Lee's name!" Manass replied with a smile.

"Really!" Mom responded.

We grew quiet as we digested this bit of information.

But why would Satan leave if you called on the name of a man? I wondered. *Didn't Wilbur Lee teach us to do this in Jesus' name?* It suddenly struck me. *Oh, he is a prophet. Of course, that's why it worked.*

Our visit that evening was short. Wilbur Lee seemed to be in good spirits, but he didn't have much to say.

"They seem to be watching extra close today," he said,

"so we must be careful what we say and how long we visit. Just remain faithful to the teachings the Father has given through me."

We left after about half an hour.

Several days later Manass stopped in again. "Did you hear that Wilbur Lee is home again?"

"No, we didn't," Mom replied. "That is good news."

A weight rolled off my chest when I heard the news. Now life could go on as before. I could hardly wait until our next visit.

* * *

Wilbur Lee shared his property with his thirty-year-old sister Mary Alice and his twenty-one-year-old brother Herman, who lived together in a trailer on the east edge of his four-acre lot. Mary Alice had been a faithful follower ever since Wilbur Lee started teaching about the Spirit's leadings. Although she had been raised in the same Amish home as her brothers, she drove a vehicle and had her hair cut and fashioned like her English neighbors. She had left home and the Amish church when she was a teenager.

Although Wilbur Lee supported the plain dress of the Amish, he didn't seem to mind Mary Alice's appearance. In fact, since she lived on the same property he did, she served as his chauffeur. It was common to see Mary Alice driving to town with Wilbur Lee in the passenger seat.

Herman also supported Wilbur Lee and followed his teachings. Because of this, Wilbur Lee chose him to be his special disciple, along with my brother Calvin.

Wilbur Lee believed the Father was revealing His true will to him. During this period of revelation, his doctrines were to be kept strictly confidential within the group. After the revelations were complete, he had a vision for spreading his doctrines abroad. He and his faithful disciples would accomplish this.

Wilbur Lee spent many hours teaching his spiritual revelations and lessons to his young disciples. Often these sessions would go late into the evening, and sometimes the boys even ended up staying the night.

"Why do you have to go for the night, Calvin?" Mom would question time and again. Calvin would only shrug his shoulders and mumble a vague response, a troubled look in his eyes.

Wilbur Lee was attending our group meetings regularly by now. One evening when we were together, he seemed burdened and extra sober.

"You may have heard that our brother Herman is no longer living with Mary Alice. He was resisting the Spirit and would not accept my teachings any longer. I have already taught you that guns are against the Father's will. Herman rebelled and purchased a BB gun. I told him he must destroy it. He refused to obey and became very angry. He threw the gun down and stomped out the door. When the gun crashed to the floor, a jolt surged through my heart. The Father revealed to me by this jolt that Herman blasphemed the Holy Spirit by the anger he showed," he stated emphatically. "There is no more hope for him. He can never be forgiven. He is eternally doomed."

I was stunned. Fear surged through me. *Being angry is serious business! I must always be loyal to the Father's will even if it means giving up everything.*

"Anger is blaspheming the Holy Ghost," Wilbur Lee

warned his obedient members. "Herman is forever lost. Be sure never to do this. If you do as I teach, you will be sure to reach paradise when the kingdom is finally and fully handed to me by the Father."

We believed him.

The Seal

It was a hot afternoon, and Calvin, Toby, and I were cleaning out the horse barn. Usually, hauling manure was not an exciting job for us Hochstetler boys, but it seemed to go faster today. The conversation naturally drifted to Wilbur Lee.

"What convinces me is his sincere way," Toby shared. "He's always talking about the Father. The Spirit reveals something to him, and he obeys. That impresses me. The other day my wind-up watch stopped. I thought, 'I'm going to ask the Spirit what time to set it to.' He told me it was 10:42, and you know, when I checked the kitchen clock it was exactly the same time."

"What I notice is that Mom and Dad aren't yelling at each other anymore," I said, throwing another forkful of manure onto the spreader. "He helped them see how it is wrong to do that. He seems to know the Bible, and he uses the Spirit as his guide. That's what convinced me. Why couldn't the church help them? If they have the same Spirit Wilbur Lee has, then they should know how to counsel their members, shouldn't they?"

"I don't know, but I'm going to stop instruction class," Calvin shared. "I just told Mom and Dad." He had been attending instruction class for church membership that summer.

"Really!" I exclaimed. "What brought that about?"

"Well, remember what Wilbur Lee taught recently, that the Father is not pleased to be called *Gott* or God, because he wants to be our Father and Lord. He is not a God who wants to consume us as it says in Hebrews 12:29 and in Revelation 1:14, where it speaks about His eyes being as a flame of fire. Instead, He is a loving Father. In the instruction class, when I repeated our standard speech that I want to make peace with *'Gott und die Gemeind'* (God and the church), I said *'Herr und die Gemeind'* (Lord and the church). The ministers asked me to say *Gott* instead of Lord. I simply refused to do as they asked. I just don't trust the ministers anymore," he said bitterly. "They don't give me the kind of teaching Wilbur Lee gives. I am going to follow Wilbur Lee from now on. There's no point in being a hypocrite."

"I don't blame you," I sympathized. "I would quit too."

That evening at the supper table, Mom announced, "Dad and I will be going to visit Alva and Elnora in Mio, Michigan. We want to share Wilbur Lee's teachings with them. We'll leave on Friday, and we should be home again by Tuesday evening. That way we can be back for the group gathering Wednesday evening."

Mom and Dad came home late Tuesday night. The next

morning after breakfast, Dad pushed back his chair and threw his right leg over his left. I saw right away something was up.

"We had a long talk with Alva and Elnora yesterday," he began, "and I had an experience on the way home I would like to share. The van was heading back home and Mom was drifting into a much-needed nap. I was deep in thought. Our conversations were bothering me. Alva does not agree with Wilbur Lee's teachings. Doubts about Wilbur Lee were going through my head. Suppose Alva is right. Is Wilbur Lee deceiving us? Is he actually coming as an angel of light? I know it will be hard to confess to the others and the church that I was wrong, but I don't want to go to hell because I am deceived!" Dad shuddered as he spoke. He knew Wilbur Lee would say that was where he would go if he denounced him.

"We were speeding southbound on US 127. I vaguely remember seeing the Harrison/Clare exit flash by. Suddenly something caught my attention and I sat up straight. There was a red light right in the middle of the windshield! It seemed impossible, so I looked closer. Leaning forward, I squinted. It was there, just as bright red as could be, about the size of a quarter. Then it disappeared.

"I shook Mom to wake her. She woke up and rubbed her eyes. 'What's wrong?' she wondered.

" 'I saw a strange red light on the windshield just a few seconds ago!' I whispered so the driver wouldn't hear me. 'It was there so plain for maybe fifteen or twenty seconds, and then it disappeared. I wonder what it means.' We both lapsed into silence.

"I suddenly realized it was a seal! That's what it was. Now it was coming together. Alva's warnings about Wilbur Lee deceiving us and this red light meant the same thing. God sent us this red light meaning that we should stop. We should stop following Wilbur Lee. That light was a sign from God. I'm convinced."

After Dad's announcement, he turned to Mom. Mom slowly nodded, her eyes downcast. "Yes, I'm afraid we were drifting from the Amish faith," she said slowly. "Wilbur Lee has many good teachings, but like Dad says, I also think this is a seal."

My stomach knotted. The silence around that breakfast table was terrible.

Calvin spoke up. "But remember all the good things that have happened to our family since Wilbur Lee began teaching us. We are happier now than we've ever been before!"

My thoughts were in turmoil. *Why is Dad so gullible? How does he know that light was from the Father? As soon as I'm on my own, I'll just go back to Wilbur Lee.* I did not trust myself to speak.

That evening the group gathered again without Wilbur Lee to discuss his latest teachings and revelations. Before the conversation progressed too far, Dad cleared his throat. "I have something important to share tonight." His voice was even and his eyes were set. "We had several long talks with Alva and Elnora earlier this week, and God showed me a sign that convinced me that Alva is right about Wilbur Lee. Alva says Wilbur Lee is deceiving us. I did not know what to think for sure, but on the way home from Mio I saw a bright red light the size of a quarter in the middle of the van's windshield. It shone for about twenty seconds, and then it disappeared. I believe God is showing us to stop. We are not going to come to these meetings or visit Wilbur Lee anymore." His voice rose, indicating the finality of the decision. He stopped his speech, breathing heavily.

The room fell stone silent, except for the heavy breathing of my agitated father. The tension was electric. No one moved; we were too shocked.

I was the first to let loose. I dropped my head into my hands, sobbing violently—great heaving sobs. My body rippled with emotion as I considered my parents' shocking declaration. My thoughts raced. *Don't they realize where they are heading? Did they forget all the truths Wilbur Lee taught them? Did they already forget how he helped us get along as a family? What do Alva and Elnora know about him? Are Mom and Dad not afraid of going to hell? They are going to burn forever and ever!*

I was not alone. Others ran out of the room, crying loudly. Manass covered his face with a large red handkerchief. Calvin was sobbing. Mom was crying softly. Even Dad was dabbing at his eyes. They had never expected such a response.

Now what would they do? Were they wrong after all? Were they being too gullible with Alva?

Then the questions came. Manass talked first. "Mom and Dad, first of all, understand that we love you, but don't you think you moved plenty fast with that decision? Remember, we spent a lot of time seeking the Father's will in this. How can you do this to us? Don't you know that you will be cast into hellfire for turning your back on the

Father? How do you know that Alva isn't deceived? Did he ever speak with Wilbur Lee?"

Dad did not answer.

"Can't you please reconsider?" I pleaded. "Did you forget all that Wilbur Lee taught us and how he helped you already? Are you just turning your backs on all that?"

"Dad, can't you see how hard this is on all the children?" asked Peter.

"Don't you think Alva and Elnora would see things differently if they visited Wilbur Lee even just once, like we did?" Sadie asked. "Don't you see all these witnesses?"

Dad's shoulders were drooping from the onslaught. He was stumped, first by the emotional response, and then by the questions. "I don't know," he admitted weakly, shaking his head. "I . . . I guess I did not look at it from all those angles. Those are all good questions that I should have been asking Alva."

Mom had said nothing so far, but her bearing suggested that her mind was changing. "Yes, I agree with you, Dad. We hadn't thought it through carefully enough."

"Would you consider talking with Wilbur Lee about this before making a decision?" Manass pleaded.

"Okay, we will talk with Wilbur Lee tomorrow night and share our doubts with him and see what he has to say about it," Dad relented.

A surge of relief swept through me. *That was close,* I thought, letting out a long, ragged sigh.

"Thank you, Dad and Mom, for letting the Spirit have His way," Manass said with evident relief.

There were more thanks, praise the Lords, and similar expressions from the much-relieved group. The conversation resumed its normal course after everyone was seated again. It was well after dark before the group disbanded that night.

The next evening found us on Wilbur Lee's doorstep. Dad cleared his throat as soon as Wilbur Lee had shown us seats. He did not waste any time in relating the story.

Wilbur Lee sat rocking slowly in his hickory rocker. "Well," he started slowly, "you may leave if you want to. You do not have to stay here under my teaching. You may make your own choices. However, you must give account to the Father for the choices you make. Just remember all the revelations the Spirit gave me already. I have been patiently teaching you, and I don't want you to forget these things. In fact, I can tell you what that red light really means," he said with a slight smile.

"Oh, really!" exclaimed Dad. "Yes, do!"

Wilbur Lee settled back and rubbed his balding forehead in deep thought. "That red light actually means that the Amish are trying to stop you. That wasn't God stopping you. It's the Amish! That's exactly what Alva and Elnora were trying to do. It happened on your way home from their place. The Father was warning you of what was happening, but you understood it completely wrong."

Dad's mouth hung open. He slowly shook his head. "Well, well," he responded sheepishly. "I can easily see what you mean. This is kind of embarrassing, but I'm sure you are right."

Mom was nodding slowly.

"Clarence," Wilbur Lee said quietly, "you must become more established in the faith before you go out and tell others about these teachings. You must leave the interpretations of these seals to me for now. You may read the Bible, but you must depend on me for interpreting it. Some texts in the Bible were actually written by Lucifer himself. The Father reveals to me which they are."

"Really! I never imagined that!" Dad exclaimed.

"But just yesterday my dad quoted this verse from Galatians 1:8, 'But though we, or an angel from heaven, preach any other gospel unto you than that which we have preached unto you, let him be accursed,'" Mom said earnestly.

"Yes, that is the perfect example! Where do curses come from? Lucifer, of course! The Father doesn't pronounce curses. That verse was written by Lucifer himself to keep you from believing the truth the Father reveals to me." He spoke smoothly and convincingly.

"I guess that makes sense," Mom said slowly.

"Yes, we will let you explain the Bible to us from now on," Dad agreed.

I let out a relieved sigh. *That was close! I wonder what we would have done if they had decided to leave?* The thought was unsettling. I was grateful that Dad was becoming convinced again that Wilbur Lee was right. I felt secure knowing we had someone much wiser than my family to interpret the Bible.

Chapter 9

Lessons

One exceptionally warm summer evening, my family decided to visit Wilbur Lee again. It had been nearly two weeks since we'd been taught by him personally.

Dad led the way to the door and knocked. Everything was silent inside. I expected to hear a cheery "come in" like usual. Dad had just reached out to knock again when the curtain parted and Wilbur Lee's face appeared in the crack. The knob rattled and the door swung open.

"Come in!" he beamed as his face took on a big smile. I followed the others inside. "Here, have some seats," he motioned. "My sister Mary Alice is visiting tonight, but you are more than welcome to join us." Mary Alice smiled as she brought some folding chairs for us.

After everyone was settled, Dad opened the conversation. "I thought you might not be home after I knocked and nobody answered right away," he chuckled.

Wilbur Lee smiled. "Yes, I know you probably did, but

the Father revealed to me that one shouldn't just say 'come in' when he hears a knock on the door."

"Really? Why shouldn't you do that?" I wondered. I was always curious about the details the Father revealed to Wilbur Lee.

Wilbur Lee's expression was somber. "You should always check before answering because it may be an evil spirit."

My heart lurched. So that was why he peered through the curtain first! This was getting interesting.

Wilbur Lee changed the subject. "I'm sure you want to hear about my trip out West. It was a real learning experience in trusting the Father and listening to the Spirit," he said smoothly.

"Sure," said Mom. "We're interested. You have so many things to teach us." We boys leaned forward in our chairs, eager to hear more.

Wilbur Lee was pleased with his followers' attention. "What I am about to tell you is foundational to our belief, so listen carefully to what I have to say," he began earnestly. "In my commitment to find more truth, I felt I needed to find the true kingdom here on this earth. I did not find it in the Amish churches. I have not found it in the Mennonite or the Protestant churches either. They all have their personal agendas. Many are set in the traditions they were taught from childhood. What I am establishing now is the true kingdom of the Father here on earth. We need an establishment that is sensitive to the Spirit of the Father; one that moves when He commands and one that cares about its members and does not grieve the Spirit.

"This was my first lesson by the Father," he said with a

faraway look. "I was led by the Spirit to visit the Mormon temple in Salt Lake City, Utah. I did not know whom I would meet or what I would find. The Spirit told me to go, so I went.

"I got Mary Alice to drive me to the bus station." He waved his hand slightly toward Mary Alice, who was sitting quietly on the other side of the room. "I told her I would be back in two weeks, and we arranged a date and time for her to pick me up," he continued. "I went to the window and got a ticket for Salt Lake City. After I boarded the bus, I felt so lonely. I really struggled. I wondered what the Father was going to teach me." Wilbur Lee's voice betrayed a slight tremble.

I noticed Mary Alice dabbing her eyes with a flower-printed hanky. A wave of soft brown hair fell across her face as she bent her head. *She must understand exactly how he felt,* I mused. *They must be really close.*

"As the bus approached Salt Lake City, I began to feel concern about getting off at the right bus stop and finding my way around this large city. I promptly felt ashamed when I realized all I needed to do was ask the Spirit for direction. So I asked the Spirit what I should do to find the correct bus station. He answered immediately!" Wilbur Lee looked triumphantly at his listeners. "The faithfulness of the Father! It is such a blessing to have such instant communication. What power! The Spirit revealed to me that I should ask loudly where the Mormon temple is. Immediately, the man sitting in front of me turned around and said he knew exactly where it was.

"I couldn't believe my eyes. Here sat a rough-looking man with long, shaggy hair. He sat somewhat twisted on his seat, and I realized he had only one leg. After I got over my surprise at my instant answer from the Father, I asked him where to get off. He told me. It was so thrilling to know that the Father cares about the little things we encounter. It just confirmed again what I already knew— that I have the true Spirit of the Father." Wilbur Lee leaned back in his hickory rocker, his balding head cocked to the left with his eyes closed, a serene look on his face.

He looks like a saint, I thought admiringly. It felt good to be in the presence of such a man of God.

Wilbur Lee faced his supporters again. "And then I was surprised to find out he was a Christian. The Father gave me a sharp lesson that day not to judge by sight whether one knows the Father. This good man told me when to get off so I could stay at a motel within walking distance of the temple.

"The next morning as I walked to the Mormon Temple Square, I was impressed by the magnificence of the temple and wanted to go inside. People milled around the entrance. As I walked to the gate leading into the temple, a young woman stopped me. She introduced herself as a missionary. After exchanging pleasantries, she said only members of the Mormon Church could enter. They went in strictly for special religious ceremonies. I told her that was fine; I had not realized it was only for members. I noticed a young man by her side, and he seemed really interested in me. They wondered if I wanted to learn more about the Mormon faith.

" 'Why, certainly,' I responded. So they spent about half an hour indoctrinating me about their various beliefs stemming from the golden book found by Joseph Smith. An angel by the name of Moroni told Joseph where to find these gold plates with a message from God. Joseph Smith became a prophet and was held by his followers to be next to the Father himself."

Wilbur Lee cleared his throat and continued. "They asked me if I believed in God. 'Of course I do,' I told them. I told them how the Father directed me out there and how the Spirit worked out the miracle on the bus. They soon realized that I was well acquainted with their Father." Wilbur Lee chuckled a bit.

"Do you think Joseph Smith was led by the same Spirit as you?" I wondered.

"I was amazed at the many examples they gave of Joseph Smith's relationship with the Father," Wilbur Lee complimented. "In his search for the truth, Joseph Smith visited many churches in all the different denominations, including the Amish and Mennonites. He was disappointed to find that none of these had the truth. He decided he must go to God in fasting and prayer for many days in an effort to find the Father's will. On September 21, 1823, he was finally rewarded by a visit from the angel Moroni in a vision. Moroni then told him where to find the gold plates.

"Joseph searched and found the plates where Moroni had told him, but they were written in a different language. The Father was faithful to Joseph and caused His Spirit to work miraculously through him to interpret the plates. He spent many months interpreting them and writing them in a language others could understand. They are now available for everybody printed in a book called the Book of Mormon."

Wilbur Lee looked piercingly at each of us by turn. "If

we want an answer from the Spirit, at times we must fast and pray."

I shifted nervously in my metal folding chair as his steady gaze rested on me.

"On my last day at Salt Lake City, I left Temple Square and returned to the motel for my suitcase. I headed for the bus station, but I was late and missed the bus. 'Now what do I do?' I wondered. The Father was faithful once more. The station was just a dinky little place, and the agent asked me to leave the building so he could close and lock the door. I didn't know what to do. It was getting dark, and it did not look like a safe neighborhood. I asked the Spirit if I should go back to the motel or just wait. He told me to wait, so I stood there and watched the traffic go by.

"I was tempted to doubt the Spirit's answer when nobody stopped or even slowed down. Suddenly a little blue car slowed and stopped. I had seen it go by a minute earlier. The man came over and asked if I had a problem. I told him I had missed the bus and was not sure what to do. He seemed friendly and told me I was not in a safe part of town. He then invited me to come to his house for the night. It turned out he was a Baptist minister. I was amazed that the Spirit worked through a Baptist who had no connection with the Mormons.

"The next day on the bus another problem occurred to me. I was getting home a day later than scheduled, and I did not have a way to let Mary Alice know about the delay. She would go to pick me up at the bus station, and I would not be there. She would have no idea what happened to me. And no one would be there for me when I arrived a day late. Again, I earnestly sought the Spirit's direction.

The Spirit told me that Mary Alice would be at the station on the right day to pick me up. Once again I resigned myself to the Spirit's power."

I listened eagerly. This was interesting. *He certainly knows how to talk to the Spirit,* I thought, gazing admiringly at my leader. I felt warm all over.

Wilbur Lee continued. "As the bus approached the Goshen station, I looked anxiously out the window, trying to spot Mary Alice's blue car. Sure enough! There it was, parked right by the gate. I just bowed my head and thanked the Father for His power!"

I glanced at Mary Alice sitting on the couch. She was smiling and nodding in agreement. "Yes," she said, "I clearly felt led to wait a day."

I shook my head in amazement. *This is definitely a prophet from God,* I thought conclusively.

"Those were some real miracles," Mom ventured.

Wilbur Lee's face glowed at the compliment. "Yes, you are right. They were very real to me. The Father chose me as His prophet just like Joseph Smith. It is important that I do whatever the Spirit tells me. He is always faithful."

He paused thoughtfully and then continued. "Although I believe Joseph Smith was truly a prophet of the Father when he started out, he began practicing things that were contrary to the Spirit, such as polygamy, and he finally fell away. There is also far too much formalism in the Mormon Church. The Spirit told me that He wants me to continue where Joseph Smith fell away. He wants me to build His true church. It is sad when men of God fall away like that," he added sadly.

"Although I don't agree with everything he taught, it is

apparent he had the Father's Spirit in the beginning. I believe we can learn from him and some of the things he practiced and taught. He was a humble and plainly dressed man of God."

Wilbur Lee paused a bit and then made a surprising statement. "The Spirit has been revealing some things recently. He revealed that all the men and boys should wear suspenders. Joseph Smith was one of the Father's great prophets, and he wore suspenders. This pleased the Father, and it will please Him to see you do the same. I know it may be difficult to begin with, but it is important. Someday you will understand it better."

I sat up straight. Had I heard correctly? Was I supposed to wear these old suspenders my whole life? My thoughts churned and I didn't hear much of the rest of the visit. I was finally almost old enough to quit wearing suspenders, and I had been looking forward to it. I saw that Toby and Calvin were struggling with this new revelation also. But I certainly didn't want to displease the Father.

It was common practice in our community for boys to wear suspenders until we graduated from school. After that, most quit wearing them, making them look more grown-up, like their older brothers and many of their fathers. We boys looked forward to this as a step of maturity. My fifteenth birthday was less than two months off. Now, if I was hearing Wilbur Lee right, I'd have to wear them for the rest of my life.

I mutely followed the others into the dark August night. It had been a long evening, and it was very late. As the horse rhythmically clip-clopped toward home, my confused thoughts tumbled through my head.

Chapter 10

Trouble at Church

That winter the Amish school I attended had its usual Christmas program planned. I did not feel like going. I had a sore throat the day before the program and complained to Mom about it.

"May I stay home from the program?" I pleaded.

"I guess if you don't feel well you may," she agreed.

So the next evening I stayed home. I lay on the couch pondering the changes that had occurred in the last year. I felt lonely thinking about my classmates in school presenting their program pieces.

Several days later Wilbur Lee spoke with Mom and Dad. He thought they should keep me out of school and finish my eighth-grade term at home. He reasoned that the Father caused my illness over the time of the program as a special sign to take me out. He said that our beliefs and those of the Amish were too far apart. Mom and Dad agreed to keep me home from school. I was relieved. Now I did not have to worry what my friends thought about my family.

Since Herman had left Wilbur Lee's group, Calvin was the only disciple left. This brought Wilbur Lee into another serious discussion with my parents. This time he requested that I be the replacement disciple. Mom and Dad seemed pleased to have two sons chosen as the prophet's closest workers. After all, these workers would assist Wilbur Lee in teaching his revelations to the world once the time was ripe.

I was excited to be Wilbur Lee's special disciple. I would need to spend many hours under his careful tutoring, and I looked forward to this. He requested that I come over to his house for the first session the following evening.

The next evening found me on Wilbur Lee's doorstep, knocking on the door. After being welcomed inside, I settled on the couch with Wilbur Lee beside me.

After some brief introductory comments, he asked me a strange question. "Did your parents ever speak to you about the facts of life?" My blank expression answered his question. "Well, let me explain," he stated, and proceeded to explain explicitly what I should have been taught from other sources.

On the way home, my heart beat fast and my face still felt flushed. I had not expected this type of teaching. What should I believe? Some of the things he had suggested did not quite seem like only "facts of life." Now what should I do? *Well, I'd better do what he says, because he is a man of God, next to the Father, and he must be right,* I decided.

Soon after that, I was invited to stay overnight with

Wilbur Lee. Mom appeared worried when Calvin and I returned home the next morning. "Aw, don't worry, Mom." I evaded her questions and slipped out the door to the barn. My stomach knotted as I thought about the sleeping arrangements the night before, but I avoided questioning my leader's actions. It was all so new, and after all, he did not seem dangerous. Of course not! He was the great revealer of the Father's will to his faithful followers.

My brother David was going steady with his girlfriend, Mary. He was also regularly attending the meetings with Wilbur Lee. Mary was putting up some resistance to this because of her father's disapproval. David spent many dates trying to convince her that Wilbur Lee was a genuine prophet and leader from God. He tried to sound convincing, but he had a hard time making it sound as spiritual as Wilbur Lee could.

Sometimes our meetings would go far into the night, even past midnight. Since David was employed at Hochstetler Siding, a local lumberyard, he was tired by evening. By midnight, his eyes were closing.

One evening Wilbur Lee woke him with a stern, "David!"

David jumped, rubbing his eyes. "I . . . I'm sorry!" he stammered. "I guess I was too tired from working all day at my job."

I had to cover my mouth to keep a snicker from escaping, glad I was not the one caught sleeping.

Wilbur Lee was serious. "I've noticed you've been falling asleep the last several meetings. This is very disrespectful to the Father. The problem is not that you are working too hard. You're actually under a curse that is making you disinterested in the Father's message. This curse must be broken."

David's head hung in shame.

A quiet group left for home that evening.

Several days later David announced to the family that he had something on his mind.

"After battling with indecision for several weeks, I decided to ask some others for counsel. I spoke with Mary's dad, the ministry, several uncles, and my brothers who are not part of the group. They all strongly recommended I leave. Mary said she is going to break off our relationship if I continue with the group. I will be living with my boss, Harley Hochstetler, for now. It's hard to leave, but I feel it is the best choice."

A lump rose in my throat when I heard David's verdict. I knew he'd been struggling and that he didn't support the group with his whole heart, but I hadn't thought he would do this! It was hard to see him being deceived; plus, I knew Wilbur Lee would not want us to speak with him anymore. I rushed to my room as tears blinded my eyes.

* * *

One April Monday morning the bishop and several ministers arrived at our house. "Oh, no! Here comes the bishop with his deceivers!" I announced from the kitchen window. I had just noticed them climbing out of the buggy.

The bishop knocked, and Dad went to answer the door. Mom and Carolyn paced nervously in the kitchen.

In a moment, Dad's head appeared in the doorway. "Mom, Carolyn, come here," he said shortly.

All was quiet except for a low murmuring coming from

the entrance. Toby and I glanced at each other. "They are probably kicking us out, don't you think?" I chuckled nervously.

"Could be," Toby agreed.

The door slammed. I looked out the window and watched the three retreating figures, heads bowed.

The door opened and Dad appeared, followed by Mom and Carolyn. His face was drawn. He sat down heavily on the closest chair. "My, they were mad!" he said, visibly shaken.

"I guess so!" Mom agreed. "Why, the bishop said they will *meit uns bist da blut rot shamt!*" (Shun us till the red blood froths!)

"That's right," Carolyn confirmed.

"Wow, I can't imagine how they can say that and call it love!" I exclaimed.

"I'd say if that's how they feel about us, then we won't have anything to do with them. That's ridiculous!" Toby exclaimed.

That evening we visited Wilbur Lee and told him the story of the excommunication. He listened sympathetically. "I want you to simply ignore the Amish from now on," Wilbur Lee instructed. "Ignoring or shunning is a sign that the door to the ark is shut. We are in the ark. We are the only ones safe. We are the only ones going to paradise when the Father calls us home. Never discuss our teachings with anyone, especially those who left our group. We are the holy ones, waiting for the return of the Father. We do not want to run any risk of being deceived."

We were happy to obey, but a sorrow hung over our hearts for those in our family who did not join us. We knew they would never be with us in Paradise. They would be lost and going to hell forever.

Chapter 11

Learning to Listen

L ife went on. We spent many long hours listening to Wilbur Lee's teachings. One afternoon Calvin and I were sitting in Wilbur Lee's living room while he taught us.

"The new kingdom is establishing now. The Father established me as his chosen prophet, next to Himself. Jesus Christ was no more than a simple prophet. The Bible says in 1 Corinthians 15:19, 'If in this life only we have hope in Christ, we are of all men most miserable.' Therefore it is the Father's plan to reveal His truths through His chosen prophet."

We absorbed his teaching. Even though it didn't always make sense, we never questioned it, especially if it sounded religious. In the beginning the teachings had Scripture references tagged to them, but after a while they rarely did. Having lost our confidence in the Amish church, we clung to our new leader without question. Our hearts were empty and longing for fulfillment.

Wilbur Lee decided it was time to teach us disciples to listen to the Spirit. One nice summer day Mary Alice and Wilbur Lee drove up to our house in her little car. Wilbur Lee came to the door and instructed me to come with him. "I need to teach you a lesson this morning," he informed me. We both piled into the back seat and started down the road.

"Now listen carefully," Wilbur Lee instructed. "This morning we will drive wherever the Spirit leads you. Just ask the Spirit if we turn at this road and if we turn left or right. Simply press your index finger down against the second one. If you can't push it, then that means yes."

I sat beside my leader, very nervous. *What if I'm wrong?* I wondered. *How will I know for sure if it feels right? Will Wilbur Lee know if I'm right?* These thoughts tumbled through my head as Wilbur Lee sat quietly beside me. We passed several crossroads, and my fingers were busy. They trembled and became slippery with perspiration. We came to a dirt road and I pressed my fingers. *Was that the right pressure? Did I press hard enough?* I questioned myself. *I have to do something! Yes, maybe that was it!* We passed the corner. On impulse I said, "Whoa, turn here!"

But Wilbur Lee interrupted. "No, the Spirit showed me differently. You are too nervous, Wil. You must let the Spirit flow."

Let the Spirit flow? I thought incredulously. *How will I ever know?*

We found ourselves entering Goshen, and out of desperation to please my master, I tried again. I thought I felt my finger stiffen. And this time Wilbur Lee did not object. Mary Alice swung the car left into a large parking area. A cluster of little stores and shops rose up in front of us. She stepped on the brakes, and we found ourselves by a small antique shop.

"Okay," Wilbur Lee announced, "let's go in and see what the Father wishes to reveal to us in here."

My job was done for now, and we followed him into the store. I could see Wilbur Lee's busy fingers as we walked down one aisle and up another. The dingy store smelled musty. *I wonder what the Spirit wants us to get in here,* I thought ruefully, wishing I could be at home, but then immediately feeling guilty for thinking such thoughts.

Wilbur Lee stopped at a display of antique dishes and selected one. It was nothing fancy, and I thought it could hardly be worth $75, but price was not an issue today—not when the Spirit directed him to purchase it. Complete obedience was the only option. He stopped again and fingered an expensive crystal bowl. It was priced at $120, and Wilbur Lee decided we'd take that one too. We walked to the counter, and Wilbur Lee paid for the dishes. I wondered where he got the money to buy expensive items like these. *He must have a bunch of money in the bank,* I thought. After we settled back into the car, Wilbur Lee turned to me again. "Wil, why don't you find a place to eat according to the Father's leading?"

My heart jumped into my throat again. This time I decided to act a bit faster. We pulled out of town and drove for about ten miles until we were nearing Elkhart. We entered town, and I pressed my finger when I saw a McDonald's sign. This time I was sure I had a signal and told Mary Alice to stop. She did, and Wilbur Lee did not object. I relaxed and began to feel like I might make a good disciple after all.

After we arrived at his house, Wilbur Lee told me to follow him into the kitchen. I wondered what he wanted to do now. "I want to show you clearly that I can communicate with the Spirit," he said. "I will ask the Father why He made me buy that $75 dish."

He sat on a chair with his head bowed, apparently in meditation. I sat on another chair, wondering what was going on in his mind. Finally, he lifted his head and said that the Spirit would not tell him why.

"Why didn't He tell you?" I inquired.

"Lucifer is interfering with the revelation. I must break a curse before the Father will reveal His purpose," he explained seriously.

"Who has this curse and why did he get it?" I half believed I had brought it on because of my poor job in speaking with the Spirit earlier in the day, and I was frightened.

"I don't always know why the curse is there or who has it; that is not always important," he explained patiently. "I will ask Him how I should break this spell." He proceeded to meditate again.

This lesson was a bit confusing to me, but it was powerful, nonetheless. I had never witnessed such a series of revelations close-up.

Wilbur Lee opened his eyes and slowly lifted his head. I could see beads of perspiration glistening on his forehead. He looked worn out.

"The Spirit revealed that I must break this dish to break the spell," he said. "I don't know why I have to do this, but the Father demands complete obedience if we are to live with Him forever."

Wow, there goes $75, I thought, surprised. Wilbur Lee opened a drawer and pulled out a hammer. He carried the dish to a cardboard box and swung the hammer. The sickening crash resounded throughout the still house. My heart thumped. My frazzled mind was spinning.

Wilbur Lee sat down again. He heaved a sigh, his body shuddering slightly. He bowed his head again.

"The Spirit says the spell is broken now and He can flow freely again. That was the purpose for buying the dish," he said with feeling. "The curse had to be broken."

I was relieved to have the curse broken and more than relieved to have this session over. Wilbur Lee went into the living room and lay on the couch. He promptly fell asleep.

* * *

Wilbur Lee would not always tell us the complete revelations. He said he would only tell what the members could handle. His mysterious air attracted us. His level of experience and knowledge seemed unattainable, so we depended totally on him for direction in our lives.

One evening at one of our group's frequent meetings, Wilbur Lee cleared his throat and announced, "I have received another revelation from the Father. The Father showed me that our earthly possessions are a hindrance on our journey toward paradise. They tie us to this earth. He showed me that we will be taken to paradise very soon and we must be prepared. Any act of disobedience will allow Lucifer to prevent the rapture from happening. Certainly the Father is almighty, but Lucifer is also very powerful. Your obedience proves that you are willing to follow the

Father. This causes Lucifer to lose power. I want you to take this purifying of earthly treasures seriously.

"Many of these earthly things are signs of pride and fleshly desire. This life is serious, and anything that takes our focus off the Father or causes us to please the flesh must go. It is wrong to possess anything that distracts us from heeding the Spirit. Some of your things give the evil spirits access into your homes. In fact, anything that has special value, such as pretty dishes, sports related items, dolls, games, and pets, has to go. Dolls are a representation of death. They look like people, but there is no life in them.

"The Father showed me that any religious symbols such as crosses and stars with circles around them are not allowed, because this will allow the spirits into your house. You are not to have any pictures on the walls. Any calendars with pictures have to be thrown out or have the pictures removed. The Scripture says in Exodus 20:4, "Thou shalt not make unto thee any graven image, or any likeness of any thing that is in heaven above, or that is in the earth beneath, or that is in the water under the earth," he finished.

My heart sank. *Do I have to give up the softball glove my parents gave me for my birthday? What about the Monopoly game our family has had all my life? How can this be sinful? What about our dog, Sport?* We were very much attached to Sport. My earliest memories included him. I clearly remembered Alva and Manass bringing home a little black and white puppy when I was only four or five years old. He was a mix of blue heeler and German shepherd. How I loved him! I hated the thought of giving him up. Sport was well trained. At our command he sailed over fences without touching them. We even trained him to bring in the cattle and horses by himself. My thoughts churned madly.

"How will this rapture take place?" inquired Manass, apparently more concerned about the rapture than I was.

Even though it was already late, Wilbur Lee eagerly leaned forward in his chair. "You will go to sleep at night as usual, and one morning you will wake up in paradise!"

This was sounding interesting again.

"Do you know exactly when this will be?" Toby asked.

"No, I don't," he responded. "But I know it will be very soon. In fact, I am working faithfully with the Father on behalf of all of you. I really struggled with telling you this revelation, because I didn't think you would believe it."

"Oh, no, Wilbur Lee! Don't feel that way for one minute. We are all in this together! We believe everything you say," Manass assured him.

"I appreciate that. It takes a great weight off me." He flashed a satisfied smile. "I'm sure you will do your best to obey the Father."

We were a sober group as we dispersed and headed home.

It was late as Toby and I got ready for bed. "I wonder if the rapture will happen tonight," I said.

"I think so," Toby said seriously. "Wilbur Lee even wrote 'THE END' on his lawn. He wouldn't do that if he didn't think it would happen soon."

"See you in paradise!" I exclaimed. I lay in bed thinking about our evening. My heart skipped a beat as I thought how this would affect the people who would be left behind. I could hardly fall asleep because of my excitement to wake up in paradise. Finally, I drifted off.

The next morning the alarm clock rattled and I woke up. *Am I in paradise?* I thought immediately. But my disappointed eyes focused on the bedroom ceiling. My heart sank. The end had not come. Not yet.

Chapter 12

Cleaning House

After dressing, I went out to do the chores. Sport ran toward me, wagging his tail, jumping up to receive a pat on the head. "Hi, Sport!" I greeted him. His eyes begged for attention. I reached down to pet him and abruptly stopped. *Oh, no! I can't pet him!* I withdrew my hand and kept on walking. I couldn't treat him as a pet. My heart ached as I looked deeply into Sport's pleading eyes. *I cannot afford to disobey the Spirit with such an earthly distraction,* I told myself. But I could not bear the hurt look in Sport's eyes. Sport sat down right in my path. He whined and scratched at my pants. "No, Sport!" I commanded, trying to be brave. Sport lay down whimpering, hurt and confused by my strange behavior.

Shortly after this, I was gone with Wilbur Lee one afternoon. When I came home, I noticed immediately that Sport was missing. Toby was doing chores in the broiler house. I approached him from behind and asked, "Toby, where is Sport?"

At first it appeared Toby hadn't heard me. Slowly he turned and faced me, a strange expression on his face. He had obviously been crying. My heart leaped to my throat. "What happened?" I demanded.

"He's gone!" Toby sighed.

"Really?" I had known Sport would have to go, but it still didn't seem real that they had actually gotten rid of him.

"That was the hardest thing I ever did!" Toby cried.

"How did you do it?" I wondered, half afraid to know.

"Well, Dad told me that since we had trash to take to the dump anyway, I might as well take Sport to the dog pound. It's right next to the dump, you know. It was the longest four-and-a-half miles I ever drove. When I turned onto 300 South, Sport crowded right up to me on the buggy seat. I'm sure he felt something wasn't right."

"Was it hard to get him into the office?" I inquired.

"No, he just followed me obediently." He shook his head as if trying to erase the scene from his mind. "The officer was nice and took him into a back room on a leash. Sport was whimpering as he went. He looked back at me with such pleading eyes . . ." Toby's voice broke.

The broiler feed room was silent as I waited for him to continue.

"As I started out the driveway, Sport must have heard the steel buggy wheels. His pitiful howls were horrible!" Toby's voice trembled.

Toby and I comforted each other with the thought that we were obeying the Spirit–that this was the right thing to do. I felt like crying, but if I did, I wouldn't be supporting what the Father had revealed. There had been no petting or hugging, no fond final words. The pain in Sport's eyes would haunt me for years.

A few days later, we had a great housecleaning day to remove any forbidden items from our home. Calvin and I used the finger pushing method to determine what we should keep or discard.

I opened the door to the attic, and we climbed the stairs to the dark, dusty room. Mom and Dad had collected many items throughout the years. Calvin and I got busy. Our flashlights exposed treasures from bygone years. We found old clothes, boxes of *Family Life* and *Blackboard Bulletin* magazines, and our old school books. Surprisingly, the Spirit told us to get rid of nearly everything in the attic. We stuffed the treasures into boxes and carried them downstairs, where we started a pile in the entrance.

After finishing the attic, we went to work in the kitchen. Many things were removed from our home that day. We transported our pile over to Manass's pole building along with the other families' forbidden items. Since playing with toys and dolls was considered wrong and pleasing to the flesh, all these things had to go. There were many sad children in our group.

The pile in the pole shed kept growing. Some things had to go without even asking the Spirit. One of these was china dishes. Wilbur Lee had informed us that china dishes were idolatry. This was difficult for Mom and the other mothers, as most of them had a set of china dishes that had been given to them by their parents or another close relative.

At the next visit, we assembled a bit despondently. For

some reason this seemed to please Wilbur Lee. "To obey the Father is the most important thing we can do. When the Father and I take you home, you will be thankful that you gave up these earthly treasures," he encouraged us.

His attempt at comfort did not lighten the atmosphere. Suddenly I saw something that made my heart lurch. There on a shelf was the crystal bowl. *What about that worthless thing?* I wanted to shout. *Here we had to give up all our vain treasures, and Wilbur Lee can have a crystal bowl that does nothing except catch the eye!*

"The color black is evil," Wilbur Lee explained. "Black represents death. Why do you think people wear black at funerals? We have life! We do not want any part of death. In fact, we are not even going to die!" Wilbur Lee promised. "We are of the elite remnant, and the Father will come soon and take us straight home."

This sounds great! I comforted myself. *I am willing to give up any earthly treasures to go home with the Father. Think about it; I won't even have to die!* Dying was a scary thought.

"What about our buggies? Those are black. Should we paint them?" Toby asked jokingly.

"When the time comes, the Father will reveal what to do with them. Don't use them more than necessary," Wilbur Lee advised. "You must not wear black clothing such as Sunday suits and shoes. You must wear brown shoes from now on. This includes the women."

Manass perked up. "We need to paint our kitchen. How do we decide what color to paint it?"

"If you need to paint your walls or furnishings, this is a good time to exercise your connection with the Spirit. He will reveal what color to make them by using the finger pushing method," he instructed us.

We went home that evening with mixed feelings. We knew we had more work ahead of us. We either had to get rid of our black objects or paint them a different color. On the other hand, we had just received a great promise that we would never have to die!

The black color revelation meant that many more everyday items had to go to the "worldly" pile or be painted a different color. Inside our houses, colors flourished. The Spirit apparently had a taste for diversity. Manass's kitchen was painted bright lavender!

* * *

We gathered at Manass's house for our next meeting. Wilbur Lee cleared his throat a bit nervously. "I wonder if some of the colors are really necessary . . ." He was looking at Manass, who quickly qualified his actions.

"The Spirit clearly showed us to paint the kitchen lavender."

Wilbur Lee dropped the subject, appearing a bit embarrassed.

"What should we do with the pile in our pole barn?" asked Manass.

"Contact the buyer at the Shipshewana flea market and sell everything," he advised. "In fact, the Spirit revealed that you can take the money you get from your stuff and purchase new bicycles. He also revealed that they must be the Schwinn brand. You must get rid of your buggies soon."

Bicycles! Had I heard right? We were not allowed to have bicycles in our Amish church. How we boys had wished for bikes! We used to ride them whenever we visited our friends who were allowed to have them. This was exciting!

I glanced around the room. Surprise was written on most of the faces.

"How will I learn to ride a bike?" Mom asked, looking concerned. "I never rode one."

Wilbur Lee's face was serious. "You may learn how to ride by starting with a three-wheeler. The Spirit revealed that bicycles will be our mode of transportation from now on. That's how we will get around in paradise."

Nobody objected further.

Two days later a number of us were at Manass's pole barn depositing the rest of our forbidden items on the pile.

"When are we going to Goshen to get the new bikes?" I wondered.

"Well, I've been thinking about this." Manass leaned against the door frame, his expression thoughtful. "I wonder if we really need to hurry and get the bikes if the Father is coming soon to get us anyway."

"That's a good thought," I responded, though I couldn't help feeling a bit disappointed. There was a murmur of consent. When the group met the following week, Manass seemed a bit stressed. At the first opportunity, he asked a little impatiently, "Wilbur Lee, you said the rapture will come very soon. I expected it to happen already. Can you tell us why it didn't?"

Wilbur Lee eyed him sharply. "I have a question." He waved his arm over his listeners, clearly agitated. "How many of you have purchased bicycles?"

The room was stone quiet. Nobody moved. Manass's

face turned red. "Well, we discussed it, and we figured there is no use to get too much in a hurry with the rapture coming so soon." His explanation sounded a bit lame.

"We who?" Wilbur Lee exploded.

"Uh, some of the group was at our place getting rid of the rest of our possessions," he hedged.

Wilbur Lee sat back in his chair with his eyes closed for a minute. His face was red and beads of sweat trickled down. I had never seen him so upset.

Suddenly he sat up and pointed his finger at us. "The Father revealed that the reason He did not come and take us home is because you disobeyed. You should have immediately gone and purchased those bicycles. Your disobedience allowed Lucifer to exercise his power, and he confronted the Father in a spiritual battle which delayed the rapture!"

We sat there, stunned.

"When the Father commands us to follow Him, we must obey Him immediately! It is your fault that we are still here." He was breathing heavily by now.

After a few minutes of silence, Manass ventured, "I'm sorry I suggested we wait to buy the bikes. I can see that was not obedience. It just seemed kind of unnecessary to spend all that money if we might not even use them very long."

Wilbur Lee didn't acknowledge his confession. "I want you all to head for Goshen sometime within the next week to purchase those bicycles. Meanwhile, I will need to intercede with the Father on your behalf to remove the curse that Lucifer placed upon you for your disobedience."

Wilbur Lee did not have much to say that evening, but sent us home with a warning to always obey promptly from now on.

Chapter 13

The Wedding

Wilbur Lee was increasingly asking for Calvin and me to spend more time with him. Usually Mary Alice was sent to pick us up. Most times, she would pick us up in the morning and drop us off the following forenoon. This happened several times per week. Quite often Dad would mutter about being too busy. I also thought he looked a lot more tired lately. I felt bad letting them work by themselves so much.

In one of our meetings Wilbur Lee reminded us again, "Do not become more involved in your work than absolutely necessary. It is still causing the rapture to be delayed."

My thoughts returned to Dad and Toby trying to keep up with the chores. I could tell Dad looked a bit uncomfortable with Wilbur Lee's admonition.

"I was just wondering if there is anything we could do differently with Calvin and Wil gone so much," Dad ventured hesitantly. "Toby and I can hardly keep up with the broiler chores plus the milking by ourselves."

"Now, Clarence," Wilbur Lee chided, "you must learn to let go of your boys. They are doing the Father's business. They must do what the Father has planned for them."

Dad looked crestfallen. I wasn't sure what to think.

Since the Father did not reveal any changes to be made with the work schedule, things went on as usual. Meanwhile, everybody waited expectantly to wake up one morning in paradise. At least we could look forward to that.

* * *

One warm August evening, the group was gathered around Wilbur Lee once again. We were all present and anxious to hear any updates on the coming rapture.

Wilbur Lee was animated. He sat forward in his chair, his arms gesticulating to emphasize his message. "I know you are wondering why the rapture hasn't come yet," he guessed correctly. "The Father and I communed for a long time this afternoon. He revealed that He would be coming very soon. We must be ready when He comes. The reason He has not appeared to take us all home to paradise is that you are not pure enough. You must be spotless before Him. You must be found worthy by your perfect obedience to the Father's will."

"Is there something we can do to become more pure?" one of the members asked anxiously.

"Certainly," Wilbur Lee replied. "You must pray more. Yes, you must pray more, and you must think less of your work. You are still too earthly minded. You must let go of the things of this world. Your work tends to distract you and attach you to this earth too much. Keep your mind filled with the things of the Father. He has a perfect plan for you, and I am here to expound His will plainly to you."

How are we supposed to make a living without thinking about our work? I wondered. Though there were certain jobs I was more than glad to forget. I was a bit confused by the message that evening, but I figured the teachings would clarify with time.

They did.

* * *

One day Wilbur Lee called a meeting.

"This morning the Father revealed that the rapture is so close . . ." He showed us with his thumb and index finger nearly touching.

All right! This is what we have been waiting for! I thought. "When is the Father coming?" I blurted.

"Just a minute!" Wilbur Lee held up his hand.

My face turned red. *That was dumb of me,* I scolded myself.

"It is coming very soon!" he reemphasized. "In fact, it is so close now that you must quit making a living. Working for a living is simply tying you down too much. You must be free to go at a moment's notice. The Father has His work for you. You must be available to work for Him."

I heard several of the men suck in their breath.

"Is that so?" Manass wondered. "How will we feed our families and pay our bills?"

"Don't worry, the Father will see to that," he consoled. "The Scripture says that He feeds the sparrows, so He will certainly care for you if you are faithful and obedient to Him."

"Should we sell the cows?" Toby wondered.

"Yes, the Father wants you to sell the cows. You may keep the broilers though," he answered.

Wow, that'll be nice! I thought happily. *No more milking!* This was sounding better all the time.

The next morning Dad pushed back his chair from the breakfast table, removed his toothpick, and said, "Toby, will you call a trucker this morning to take the cows to the Shipshewana sale barn tomorrow? I want you boys to clean them up a bit this morning after you milk."

"Oh, they'll be going that soon?" I responded, surprised at the urgency.

"Yes. When the Father commands us to do something, we must obey right away," Mom put in. "We have been too slow in the past. This is one reason the Father hasn't come to take us to paradise already."

"Yes, I'd say you're right," agreed Toby. "We must obey immediately."

The following day a trucker hauled our twenty dairy cows to the sale barn.

"May we go to the sale barn and watch them sell?" I asked Dad while waiting for the cattle truck.

Dad paused a bit before answering. "No, I don't think we should. We must be careful not to mingle with the Amish yet; we need to become more established in the Father's teachings before we associate with them too much."

I knew he was thinking about their episode with Alva and Elnora. Wilbur Lee had made it clear that we were to remain to ourselves for a while, at least. I couldn't help feeling a surge of loneliness.

* * *

One day in September I saw my brother David riding out the lane in his buggy. I had been feeding the horses and was watching from the barn. I ran for the house to find out what he wanted.

Stepping inside, I found Dad, Mom, Toby, and Carolyn sitting around the table in a serious discussion. They didn't even look up when I entered.

"What did David want?" I interrupted the conversation.

Mom looked up, clearly troubled. "David and Mary are getting married in two weeks. He just pleaded that we would come to their wedding. They want Toby to be a special server for the bridal table."

Suddenly I understood Mom's expression. "Do you think we can go?" I ventured cautiously. In my heart I already knew the answer. I was turning sixteen in October. This might have been my first chance to be a table waiter. My heart sank in disappointment. *I really wish I could take part in the wedding,* I thought, *but I know we have something better to look forward to.* I looked at Toby and saw that he was struggling too.

"This would be the first time I'd be taking part in a wedding." Toby looked hopeful. "What will people think if we don't go?"

Mom looked at Dad. "What do you think?" she asked.

"Well, we can ask Wilbur Lee tomorrow evening at the meeting," Dad said. "We will do whatever the Father reveals."

The next evening we gathered at Manass's house for the meeting. Dad didn't waste any time getting to the point. "David stopped in yesterday and wondered if we are planning to attend their wedding in two weeks."

I saw Manass nodding. "Yes, David stopped in here too," Manass said.

"We were wondering if we should go to the wedding." Dad looked at Wilbur Lee. I thought I noticed a hopeful tone in his voice.

Everything got quiet as Wilbur Lee contemplated this new problem. "Let me consult with the Father," he answered. He looked heavenward and his lips moved as he worked his fingers.

Nobody spoke.

After a few minutes, he focused on us again. He sat in his rocker, leaning forward with his arms spread apart.

"Yes," he said slowly, "you may go. I am not keeping you by force. This is not a cult. You may make your own decisions. But understand that you are going to be attacked by the Amish. They will corner you and interrogate you with hard questions. You may not be strong enough to answer them. You have the truth now, but if they persuade you, the Holy Spirit will forsake you. Do you remember what happened, Clarence and Ada, when you visited Alva and Elnora in Mio? You thought you were strong, but Lucifer had you for a little while, till I rescued you. You will run a serious risk of blaspheming the Holy Spirit."

My heart fell. *But it is more important to do what the Father wishes,* I consoled myself.

"The Amish are out to deceive you," Wilbur Lee said. "You must be careful not to listen to their persuading."

Manass cleared his throat. "Yes, Mom, it is hard not to go, but we want what is best for us. It is more important to stay close to the Father. We do not want to enter into any unnecessary temptations."

"That's right," Wilbur Lee affirmed. "It is not worth the risk of losing eternal life just for some earthly pleasure. We are very close to the rapture. The Father just revealed to me this morning that it won't be long now.

"Also, the Father has given a difficult revelation that I was waiting to reveal until the Father sees you are ready to accept it." He lowered his head in meditation.

The room filled with tension.

"I will counsel the married couples separately," he announced. This was nothing new. The rocking chair creaked as he stood up and invited my parents to enter the bedroom first. They followed obediently.

There was not much discussion among the rest of us as we waited.

After fifteen minutes, Mom and Dad returned. Mom motioned to Manass and Wilma. "He wants to see you next." My heart thumped wildly.

After the meeting, Calvin and I went home with Wilbur Lee and Mary Alice.

The next morning the four of us sat in the living room discussing the meeting. Wilbur Lee leaned back in his rocking chair, crossed his legs, and chuckled.

"What's so funny, Wilbur Lee?" I asked innocently.

"Oh, I was just remembering the looks on their faces when I told them the message." Wilbur Lee slapped his knee and laughed heartily.

"What message?" I inquired.

"Aww, it was just that the Father does not want the married couples to have marital relations anymore. They are to remain celibate."

My face turned crimson. Now I better understood our sleeping arrangement.

"Are we never to marry?" I asked cautiously.

Wilbur Lee sat up straight, his face turning serious. "We are in times similar to those of Noah in the Bible. For in the days before the flood they were eating and drinking, marrying and giving in marriage, until the day Noah entered the ark. The Amish court and marry, just like in those days. The Father does not want to tempt us with marriage."

My heart sank, but I didn't dare show it. "What about those who are married now? Do they have to separate?"

"Those who are married will remain together; however, when we get to paradise, there will be no marriage. In fact, the women will transform into men."

"Oh," was all I could muster. The three of us were giving him our full attention.

"The Bible claims we were created from dust. Imagine the dust billowing out of Adam's mouth and ears when God blew into his nose. Hah!" he laughed, his hands waving in imitation.

"Now, let me explain what the Father revealed to me about how mankind was created," he stated seriously. "Originally, the Father created a plant from which Adam eventually evolved. Paradise was a beautiful and grand place where Adam lived."

Wilbur Lee went into great detail for nearly an hour describing the beauty of paradise.

"When Lucifer fell, he took this plant and changed it into a hybrid plant and produced a woman, which was Eve, after his design. She approached Adam, tempting him to eat the forbidden fruit. Because of that, they were driven out of paradise. From that day on the human race has been deceived. Because the woman was designed by Lucifer, we should not marry. The consolation for the women of our group is that when we enter paradise they will be changed into the Father's original design."

I nodded soberly, trying to digest this information.

* * *

Several days later at the breakfast table Dad nervously cleared his throat and spoke. "Mom and I discussed David's wedding. We decided not to go because we feel the Amish will deceive us."

I looked at Mom and noticed a tear sliding down her cheek. Dad didn't show too much emotion.

I was disappointed, but I was also glad I did not have to face those who would be sure to confront us. I knew the Amish thought we were weird. I was so glad we had the truth.

The day of the wedding dawned clear and beautiful. Nobody spoke at the breakfast table. Mom only picked at her scrambled eggs. I was not hungry either. Our minds were at the wedding. What would the Amish say when they saw we did not attend? After breakfast we went to finish the chores.

"Wil, could you go to Lambright Hatchery and get some chicken feed?" Dad asked.

"Sure," I responded, glad for the opportunity to get my mind on something else.

I hitched the horse to our single buggy with a two-wheeled trailer in tow and headed off. I bought the feed, and after I had paid, I led Prince around the back to the warehouse to load.

"Hello, Wil!"

I looked up in surprise. It was my cousin Paul from Michigan. "I didn't realize you worked here!" I responded. "How long have you been living down here?" I noticed he did not wear plain clothes and his hair was cut short. *He must be sowing his wild oats,* I thought.

"Oh, about two weeks now," he responded with a quizzical expression. "Why aren't you at your brother's wedding?" he demanded.

My face turned red. What was I supposed to say? I ended up ignoring his question.

"It's not right that you don't attend your brother's wedding," he insisted.

"Well, why didn't you go?" I responded, agitated.

"I'm going to go tonight," he justified himself. "But you should be there today. Didn't your mom and dad go either?" He looked upset.

"It's really none of your business," I returned heatedly. "And besides, if the Amish are so great, then why did *you* leave them?" I attempted to get the focus off me.

"At least I'd go to my brother's wedding," he retorted.

By now Paul had the feed loaded and I climbed on the buggy, slapped Prince across the back with the reins, and was on my way, anger simmering under the surface. *I guess this is what Wilbur Lee prophesied about us being persecuted. This is just a price to pay for following the Father. At least we have something better,* I consoled myself.

Chapter 14

The Bus

Calvin, Mary Alice, and I were sitting in Wilbur Lee's living room one cold afternoon. We had seen the season's first snowflakes. The trees were nearly bare, and it felt good to be in a warm house.

We watched him as he paced the floor animatedly, communicating with the Spirit. I glanced at the clock. It was three o'clock already. Wilbur Lee had been communicating since one o'clock.

We had been at Wilbur Lee's house overnight. Around ten that morning, Mary Alice had driven all of us to Goshen to do some shopping. We had been performing another lesson from the Spirit. We had stopped at the mall. After wandering through several stores following Wilbur Lee's leading of the Spirit, we finally found ourselves in a bookstore. Wilbur Lee stopped at one of the bookshelves. He pulled a heavy hardcover book off the shelf. It had a picture of a large bus on the cover. After wandering through the store for twenty minutes, he pulled another book off the shelf. I glanced at the title and saw it said something about paradise and Hawaii. *I sure wonder what the Spirit has in mind here. Maybe we'll be going to Hawaii!* I thought excitedly.

After leaving the mall, we stopped at Wendy's, Wilbur Lee's favorite restaurant, for lunch. As I was eating my delicious hamburger, I was struck by an oddity. *I wonder why we can eat these sandwiches, yet Wilbur Lee discourages eating bread? Who knows, maybe the Spirit doesn't mind restaurant bread!* I felt a tad rebellious when I thought how much I missed our forbidden pizza.

We arrived home a little before one o'clock and sat in the living room to see what the Father wanted to communicate to us through Wilbur Lee. I couldn't help but wonder what those books meant that the Spirit had us purchase. I saw them lying on the coffee table.

Wilbur Lee was concentrating on his dialogue with the Father. The floor creaked as he paced the length of the living room. He spoke earnestly, totally absorbed in his one-sided conversation. His question was pointed. "Why is the rapture not happening?"

He paused and looked at us. He had an answer. "Lucifer is angry that people actually found the truth. Because people are following the Father, Lucifer is preventing the rapture.

"This is why it is so important that we faithfully obey in all the lessons that the Father has us perform," he continued. As it says in Corinthians, 'But God hath chosen the foolish things of the world to confound the wise.' We don't understand everything the Father asks us to do, but

He has something He wants to show us."

Wilbur Lee bent down to pick up his new books off the coffee table. "Father, why did you want me to buy these two books today?" he inquired. "Which book do you want to talk about first? The paradise book?" He checked with his finger. The answer was negative. "Do you want to talk about the bus book?" The finger remained strong. It was clear; the Father wished to talk about the bus book. "Should I buy a bus?" His finger fell.

I was fascinated.

"Should I connect the bus to the paradise book?" His finger was strong. He slowed his pace and lowered his eyes. He was quiet for a few minutes. Finally, he raised his head and delivered the Father's revelation. "The Father spoke to me and said that because of your obedience to me today, Lucifer lost his power. Now I can come in person to pick up you, my faithful followers, with a bus and transport you alive to paradise. You will never have to die."

Wow! Just like Elijah! I thought excitedly. I was pleased that I was included. My thoughts flitted to my cousin Paul, and my chest swelled with pride. He would pay for his persecution.

"But the group won't believe me!" he countered the Spirit. "So you said those who don't believe will stay behind?" His finger affirmed this.

That evening we went to the meeting with anticipation. I was half afraid of the group's reaction when they heard this new revelation.

After everybody gathered in the living room, Wilbur Lee got right to the point. "This afternoon the Father revealed that, because of my obedience to His test, Lucifer lost his power. This morning we went shopping and the Father asked me to buy two books. One was about buses and the other one about paradise. I simply couldn't understand why He did this. Then He faithfully revealed His will for us. In fact, there will not be a rapture after all."

I heard some gasps.

"No, there won't be a rapture. He is coming in person to get us. Yes, He's coming in a bus to pick us up!"

Everybody let out a sigh of relief. A few even chuckled.

"I was afraid some of you wouldn't believe this," he continued seriously. "I told the Father my fears. He answered me that those who do not believe will be left behind. Yes, left behind," he stated soberly. "The Father revealed further that we must prove our faith in Him by quitting our jobs and relying solely on Him to meet our needs."

The room fell silent. No more chuckles. I could have heard a pin drop.

"Actually, you really won't have that many needs anyway, because the Father will come very soon. It won't be long until He comes," he consoled us quickly. "You will now be transported alive to paradise. In fact, the Father promised that those who are faithful will never have to die."

Manass was the first to speak up. "This sounds serious, and we certainly want to do everything we can to be prepared and prove our faithfulness."

Ellen spoke next. "Our daughter Amy is coming to the truth. She lives just down the road from us, and she comes to visit frequently. She is ready to join us, and I sure don't want her to miss the bus! However, her husband does not want her to join. He doesn't even want her to visit us. Our neighbors report it to her husband if they see her coming. It is very sad. They had marriage problems already, and this is making it worse." She shook her head and her voice trembled. "Wilbur Lee, could you please sit down and talk with Amy?" she finished.

"Certainly. I'll be glad to go see her," he agreed compassionately. "In fact, why don't we have a day of fasting and prayer so the Spirit can have His way?"

Chapter 15

Amy

March came around with its warming days. The trees were budding and the birds were singing. Spring was in the air.

One Sunday we met at Melvin and Ellen's house for our biweekly morning meeting. Amy was coming to our meetings regularly by now.

"I would like to announce to the group this morning," Wilbur Lee began, "that the Father revealed that Amy should not be living with her husband Michael anymore, since he does not support our group. She has been living with her parents since Thursday."

"We are glad for Amy that she does not have to live under her husband's rule anymore and risk being deceived," added Ellen.

We nodded in agreement.

"I am thankful that you support me like this," Amy added, relief written on her face. "You would not believe the pressure Michael put on me to come back, but I am determined not to return. It is not easy, because two of the children are still with him."

What a strong woman, I thought, *to sacrifice her marriage for the sake of the truth.*

* * *

Mary Alice spun in the drive, tooting the horn. She jumped out and burst through our door, forgetting to knock, her face flushed with excitement. "Michael kidnapped Amy today. We have no idea where she is. We must meet tonight at Melvin and Ellen's house."

"Oh, Mary Alice, what happened?" Mom asked in alarm. "Do you think Amy is all right? What are we going to do?"

"I don't know. I just feel so helpless," Mary Alice answered. Her hand trembled as she brushed a tear from her cheek. "I gotta run. I have to let the others know about the meeting."

She turned and ran out the door. The car door slammed and she was gone.

Mom looked at us with wide eyes. "What should we do?"

"I have no idea," I said as I leaned heavily against the kitchen sink. "I guess we will find out tonight."

That night at the meeting, we gathered in a large circle. Our faces were drawn and tense.

Ellen looked distraught as she began her story. "It was around seven in the morning when we heard someone knock on the front door and Amy went to answer. It was Michael. He told her he just wanted to speak with her for a few minutes. She went out the door and he started talking, walking toward the car he had come in. We should have thought it strange that he came in a car since he lives only a quarter mile from us. Anyway, we didn't think that far, and the next thing we knew he grabbed her around the waist and half dragged her to the car. Amy looked over her shoulder and screamed, 'Mom, Dad, help me! Pleeease!' " Ellen dropped her face into her hands, and her shoulders shook with sobs.

We were stunned.

"When I heard the screaming, I ran from the barn, but I was too late." Melvin resumed the story. "I saw Michael push her into the back seat and climb in beside her, and the car spun out the drive. A friend passing by saw the commotion and swung in. We discussed what happened and he immediately offered to call the police. Meanwhile, our son Elam jumped on his bike and notified Wilbur Lee. The police arrived in about ten minutes. We discussed what to do, and the police requested a photo of Amy. They want to show it on national television. Of course, we don't have pictures, but a neighbor was able to locate one for us."

For two weeks the group waited anxiously for news. Finally, Mary Alice received a telephone call late one evening from the LaGrange County Sheriff's Department informing her that Amy was in southern Illinois. They offered to bring her back home to her parents.

A few days later we again met at Melvin and Ellen's house. When I saw Amy sitting in the living room with the rest of the group, a surge of relief swept through me.

Amy was the center of attention as she recounted her experience. "After Michael had me in the car, I saw a large man in the seat beside the driver. Then I was blindfolded so I couldn't see where they were taking me. We traveled for what seemed like hours and hours until we entered a busy city. I could hear lots of traffic all around me, but I couldn't see anything. Finally, the car stopped and Michael guided me into a building. We walked a while and turned a number of corners. When we stopped, I heard a door latch and the lock click shut. The blindfold was finally taken off."

"Where were you?" Mom wondered.

"I found out later that I was in some building in Chicago," she explained. "They brought me to this man who asked me question after question. He was some kind of cult counselor Michael had contacted for help. This man and Michael and the friend who had helped him kidnap me explained that I was brainwashed and that they needed to deprogram me. I simply refused to give any information. I was there for several days. Finally, I cooperated a bit and they decided to take me to Michael's parents' place in southern Illinois."

"How did you escape?" Manass asked.

"Well, I cooperated with them more and more, and one day I asked if I could go for a walk. I had gone on walks before, so they didn't object. I started walking down the road toward the neighbors' house. When I got out of sight of my in-laws' house, I dashed to the neighbors'. They were sitting outside on lawn chairs, and I asked them if I could use their phone to call the police. They refused to let me at first, saying they didn't want to get involved. But I kept insisting. Finally, they let me in and I found the phone. When I looked out the door, the couple was driving out the lane.

"I dialed 911 and said, 'I've been kidnapped and I need help.' In no time the police were out and picked me up. The police then took me to the station until the LaGrange County police came to bring me home. It was awful the way Michael treated me."

Numerous clucks and i-yi-yi's were heard around the room as we shook our heads in sympathy.

"What happened to Michael and the men who kidnapped you?" Manass inquired.

"The police arrested all three of them. Now they are sitting in jail, and I don't know what will happen to them."

Three days later I was at Wilbur Lee's house when a car drove in the lane and a man in a suit climbed out and knocked on the door. Wilbur Lee stepped outside to talk to him.

After a while Wilbur Lee walked back in with a disturbed look on his face.

"Who was that man and what did he want?" I asked.

"Michael's lawyer," he answered shortly.

"Really! What did he have to say?"

"He basically told me that if Amy presses charges, he will try to make me look bad," Wilbur Lee spoke quietly.

"What will you tell Amy to do?"

"I will ask the Father what we should do."

That afternoon Wilbur Lee communicated with the Father, and He revealed that they should not press charges.

The case was dropped.

Chapter 16

More Lessons

By now, Calvin and I were living at Wilbur Lee's place for longer periods of time. Wilbur Lee encouraged us to communicate more with the Spirit ourselves.

"Wil, we will be going to the local greenhouse to buy flowers for the rock garden out by the road. I want you and Calvin to ask the Spirit to choose the flowers and shrubs," Wilbur Lee said.

We walked through the greenhouse looking at the many beautiful flowers and enjoying the serene setting and the refreshing smells. I began to use the finger pressing method to ask the Spirit which flowers I should purchase.

But for some reason today there was no signal from the Father. I was becoming frustrated, so I asked Wilbur Lee, "What is wrong that I am not connecting?"

"Let me consult with the Father," Wilbur Lee said. He wandered inconspicuously among the rows of plants, his lips scarcely moving. Shortly he approached from behind and lightly touched my left elbow. I turned slowly and looked him in the face.

"Lucifer put a block between you and the Father," he explained softly. "I interceded on your behalf, but the Father wants you to recognize the block. Your obedience to the Spirit in resuming your search for the right plants will open the connection between you and the Father."

"Oh, yes, that makes sense," I said, relieved. "I will try again. I'm sure I can do it now." With that, I walked through the rows of plants diligently pressing my fingers. Now I could feel the connection. *Go to row eight* flashed through my mind. Was that from the Father? "Do you want me to go to row eight?" I whispered under my breath. My finger stayed strong, which meant yes.

Row eight contained beautiful rosebushes. "Should I choose this red one?" I whispered. My answer was no. Next, I went to the peach rosebush. This time the answer was yes. This process continued until we made all the selections for the rock garden.

That afternoon I consulted the Spirit for the placement of the plants. I felt thrilled and empowered by my direct connection with the Father.

About a month later, Wilbur Lee's sister stopped in to break the sad news that their dad had died. It was June 23, 1990. We had known that he was in the hospital because of a heart attack, but we had not expected this.

After his sister left, I asked, "Are you going to attend the funeral?"

"Well, I don't know," Wilbur Lee said uncertainly. "I will need to ask the Father."

On the morning of the funeral he announced, "The Father does not want me to go the funeral. We will need to stay away from here today, because people might stop in to harass us."

I had expected this. We loaded into Mary Alice's car and drove to town. We went shopping and then headed to the park for the rest of the afternoon. After eating supper at a restaurant, we found a motel for the night.

A week later one of Wilbur Lee's friends stopped in to visit a bit. "Did you realize that several Amish men were at the funeral waiting for you? They had planned to corner you and take you to Oaklawn by force."

Wilbur Lee gasped. "I felt led by the Holy Spirit not to go."

This is definitely a seal from the Father, I thought. *The Father certainly protected us.*

"I can't blame you for not being there." His friend shook his head in sympathy. "You know, I overheard two ladies talking the other day. They claimed you could move furniture just by waving your hands."

Wilbur Lee laughed and said, "Sure, I can move furniture with my hands." With that, he lifted one end of the table. We all laughed.

"Another thing people say is that you are going to isolate your group like Jim Jones did," he said, shaking his head in disbelief. "Not only that, people are saying you made a grave in your garden."

Wilbur Lee shook his head sadly. "The Amish love to gossip. If only they would understand the truth . . ."

* * *

"I was just wondering how we should handle our finances," Manass said slowly. "I don't want to complain, but, well, with the bus not showing up yet and quitting our jobs, it's kind of hard to buy groceries." His face had turned red.

We were meeting at Melvin Miller's house that October night. The room fell silent, and I could feel the tension rising. *Manass sure has nerve,* I thought.

"You don't realize how hard I have been working on your behalf with the spirit world," said Wilbur Lee. "Your impatience is making it much harder to resolve this. Lucifer puts up blocks because of your attitudes." He sounded a bit impatient himself. "In fact, the Father knew you were going to ask this question, so He gave me the answer this afternoon already."

"I'm sorry for not trusting the Father to provide. I'm anxious to hear your answer," Manass said humbly.

Wilbur Lee leaned forward in his chair. "The Father will be coming soon with His bus, so it is unnecessary to own excess property. The Father revealed to me that you must sell whatever land you don't need and use that money for living expenses."

"Sure, that makes sense," Manass agreed. "We have thirty acres in the back we could sell."

The others joined in, offering to sell large sections of their properties.

"I will even sell my property that Mary Alice's trailer is on. She can move in with me," Wilbur Lee offered. Mary Alice nodded in approval.

There was a lively discussion as everybody planned how to split their properties. It was late when we finally arose to leave. I was just going out the door when my sister Elsie called out, "Happy seventeenth birthday, Wil!"

"Thanks, I nearly forgot!" I responded with a laugh.

* * *

It was January 1991, and Grandpa Miller, Mom's dad, was very low with cancer. On the morning of the tenth, we got word that he had passed away. We sat around the kitchen table trying to digest the news. I could see that Mom was sad, though she did not cry.

"What will people think if we don't go to the funeral?" Mom asked worriedly.

"But Mom, you know the people will just try to deceive us at the funeral," I reminded her.

"Yeah, and people will think we are weird if they see us wearing brown shoes and no Sunday clothes," added Toby.

Two days later the funeral was held at Uncle Amos's place, just a quarter mile down the road. We decided to go to Melvin and Ellen's house for the day to avoid the crowd. The day passed uneventfully.

The next day Mom's brother Menno from Michigan stopped in for a visit. After he was seated in the living room, he looked at Mom and said with feeling, "We really missed you at the funeral."

Mom fidgeted with the handkerchief in her hand. Everyone was quiet. Finally, Dad broke the silence. "Were there a lot of people at the funeral?"

"Around four hundred. How come none of you were there?" Menno asked with a pained expression.

"Well, they excommunicated us, so we decided they

don't want us there," Dad said bitterly.

"But that's not true," Menno refuted. "I wish things could just be the way they used to be. Why couldn't you be there for Mom's sake in spite of our differences?"

Mom looked up with tears in her eyes. "You just don't understand."

In the silence that followed, Menno shook his head. "I guess not," he finally admitted.

Chapter 17

The Secret

It was June again, with the grass growing green and the sun shining hot. The birds were raising their young and everything seemed peaceful.

Wilbur Lee, Mary Alice, Calvin, and I had just returned from a big shopping trip in Kalamazoo, Michigan. We unloaded our many purchases, including, of all things, a large stereo.

"Now I know we were not used to stereos when we were Amish, so I don't want the others to know about this just yet," Wilbur Lee warned us after we had it set up.

I wonder why he is afraid of the others' reactions if he is only obeying the Father, I asked myself.

Later, Calvin, Mary Alice, and I were sitting in Wilbur Lee's living room while he communicated with the Father.

"Father, why did you command me to spend all this money on all this stuff?" He sounded agitated. "You made me buy this big generator, this stereo system, and a television set. Where will I get the money to buy my groceries?"

I looked up in surprise. I hadn't known we were low in money. Wilbur Lee looked stressed.

Wilbur Lee was pacing the floor, his arms swinging animatedly and his lips moving silently. Suddenly his face relaxed and he focused his attention on us again.

"The Father was faithful. He has revealed what to do." He looked directly at Calvin and said, "I want you and Wil to go home and ask your parents for thirty thousand dollars immediately."

We nodded obediently and left for my parents' house with Mary Alice. Calvin and I exchanged a nervous glance as we turned into the drive and stopped in front of the house. We climbed out of the car and slowly made our way up the sidewalk.

Mom and Dad welcomed us warmly. We seated ourselves in the living room and discussed the latest rumors flying around the community about our group.

Calvin cleared his throat and started in. "Dad, the Father revealed to Wilbur Lee that in order to sustain Wilbur Lee and his calling, we need more money."

Dad looked at Mom uneasily. "What does he do with the money all of us are giving him?"

So, this isn't the first time he's asked for money! I thought uncomfortably of the expensive dishes and the new stereo. *Who paid for those?*

Dad looked back to me. "How much money do you need?"

Calvin shifted in his chair and looked at me. Now it was my turn to be nervous. I explained as confidently as I could, "This is very necessary and is for a vital cause. The Father revealed that He needs only thirty thousand."

Everything went silent. Dad's face clouded. He opened his mouth, but shut it again without speaking. He sat still for a while, then slowly rose and walked toward the desk for the checkbook. A minute later he returned with the check in his hand.

My heart leaped with relief. Dad gave the check to Calvin. We made some more small talk and then rose to leave.

"I'm sure you will be rewarded for obeying the Father," I consoled my distraught parents.

Mom nodded. "Yes, we must be willing to give up everything if we want to go with the Father to paradise."

When we got back to Wilbur Lee's house, he took the money with a smile. "Thank you, my faithful disciples," he praised us.

"You're welcome," we responded in unison, glad to have pleased our leader.

The next morning as Wilbur Lee was getting ready to leave, he asked me, "Wil, could you get the tiller and work up the garden patch again while Mary Alice and I go to the bank?"

"Yes, I guess so," I answered a bit unwillingly.

I had just done this job a week ago, so I was surprised that he wanted it done again. In fact, I had been tilling his gardens for the past three weeks already. Often when we went to town, I asked him if he was ready to buy seed, but he always said the Spirit told him to wait because someone was disobedient. It was getting to be quite frustrating and depressing to till empty gardens all the time, especially long after other gardens were planted.

I set to work with the tiller. The garden plot was next to the busy blacktop road. It was embarrassing to be working a fruitless garden with horses clip-clopping by. I did not dare look to see if I recognized any of the passersby. I was doing something worthless, and I certainly did not care to be noticed by someone I knew.

I hate tilling this patch, but I do not want to spoil something in the spirit world, I thought.

A week later, I found myself once again tilling our fruitless garden. Mary Alice was busy with the flowerbeds while Calvin mowed the yard and Wilbur Lee attended to other yard maintenance.

Suddenly I saw Mom and Dad drive in the lane. I met them at the front walk and welcomed them warmly. "Come in! Let's sit inside and visit a while." I gestured to the door. I opened it and stepped inside. Immediately I sensed something different. What was it? I forgot my visitors temporarily, trying to figure out what was wrong. *Oh, the stereo! It's gone!* I could not believe my eyes! How had that happened so quickly?

Suddenly Wilbur Lee popped out of the bedroom, a big smile on his face. "Come in, come in!" he invited cordially. We all sat in the living room and had a nice visit. I felt uncomfortable all the while.

After they left, Wilbur Lee turned and faced me. His smile was gone. "Didn't you think about the stereo? You almost gave Lucifer power again. Where is your love for the Father? You should have come in, put the stereo away, and then invited them in. But no! You just said, 'Come on in, come on in!' In fact, you made them come in faster than they would have normally. I just barely had time to come in the back door and hide the thing." He spat the words in my face. His face was red with anger and he was breathing heavily.

I sat on the couch, stunned. I didn't dare move. I had never seen him so angry. "I . . . I forgot about the stereo," I stammered, nearly in tears.

Wilbur Lee relented. "Well, from now on you must think ahead before you do something."

"I'm sorry. I will try to do better next time," I apologized.

"You can go and finish the garden now." He ended the discussion.

I turned away, tears pushing at my eyelids.

Chapter 18

Foretelling the End

B y now, Calvin and I lived with Wilbur Lee full-time. It was a beautiful September day and we were traveling up to Holland, Michigan. Holland was a clean and well-organized city with vibrant tulip fields blooming in the spring. We enjoyed frequent shopping excursions there.

We stopped at a large mall as the Father directed and wandered into a gift shop and browsed around. We came upon some large jeweled ostrich eggs fashioned into jewelry boxes, complete with little stands. Wilbur Lee stopped and consulted with the Father, using his fingers. He nodded and picked one up. I was startled when I saw the price. *One hundred and fifteen dollars is a lot of money,* I thought. *I wonder what he wants with that thing.*

I could not help but feel a bit irritated when I thought about my parents' hard-earned money being spent on such expensive, frivolous items.

Why?

We paid for the ostrich egg and left. It was late as we neared home on US Highway 20. Wilbur Lee was driving this time. I could tell he was nervous because he did not have a license. Suddenly red and blue lights flashed behind us.

"Oh, no," Wilbur Lee groaned.

The police officer walked up to the car with a flashlight in his hand and peered into the window.

"Did you know your one headlight is out?"

"Yes, I did. I was going to fix it tomorrow."

"License and registration, please," he demanded.

Wilbur Lee reached over into the glove box, pulled out the registration, and handed it to the police officer.

"I need your license too."

"I am just learning to drive, and I don't have a license."

"I need to see you in my car."

Ten minutes later Wilbur Lee returned and motioned Mary Alice into the driver's seat.

After we were on our way, I asked, "Did you get a ticket?"

"Yes, I did. I tried to explain that I have repeatedly attempted to get a license but always failed the exam. He told me I would need to explain that to the judge, and he gave me a ticket anyway."

"That was a neat way to handle it," I remarked, though I knew he was lying about the exams.

Several weeks later Wilbur Lee had to appear in front of the judge. When Wilbur Lee and Mary Alice returned from court, we sat down in the living room. Wilbur Lee turned triumphantly to Calvin and me and said, "This morning before we left, the Father told me that the judge would not require me to get a license since that is not His will. When I stood before the judge, I explained that I had repeatedly attempted to pass an exam, but failed every time. The judge told me that if I pass an exam and appear before him with the results, I don't have to pay the ticket."

Throughout the next several weeks, Wilbur Lee studied for the exam. He passed it successfully. When he brought the results before the judge, he was acquitted. But in accordance with the Father's instructions, he did not get his license.

* * *

One morning we were seated in the living room earlier than usual. Wilbur Lee told us that the Father had commanded us to watch the sun come up. "The Father has a revelation for us," he stated. All was quiet as we watched the sun for the next half hour.

"The Father revealed to me that the sun will lose its shine, as it says in Acts. 'And it shall come to pass in the last days, saith God, I will pour out of my Spirit upon all flesh: and your sons and your daughters shall prophesy, and your young men shall see visions, and your old men shall dream dreams: and on my servants and on my handmaidens I will pour out in those days of my Spirit; and they shall prophesy: and I will shew wonders in heaven above, and signs in the earth beneath; blood, and fire, and vapour of smoke: The sun shall be turned into darkness, and the moon into blood, before that great and notable day of the Lord come.'

"This will be the end of the world, and I will be the judge. All the unbelievers will be cast into outer darkness, and we will inherit the earth," he concluded.

"When will this happen?" I asked. It all sounded a little scary, even though I knew we were going to paradise.

"Next Wednesday," he prophesied.

"Really!" I exclaimed. "We had better be ready." I glanced out the window at the sun. It still looked very bright.

That evening the group gathered again. Wilbur Lee began his warning. "The Father revealed that the end will come very soon. But before the end, the sun will lose its shine. When that happens all the unbelievers will be cast into outer darkness where there will be horrible torture and pain. The darkness will be so heavy you will be able to feel it. I will be the judge on that last day. Those who were once enlightened and returned to their old way of life will have ten times the torment in hell. Once the unbelievers are cast into darkness, we will inherit the earth. Again, this will happen very, very soon."

Shivers raced up and down my back. *Why doesn't he just tell them it will be next Wednesday?* I thought. *I wonder if it really will happen then . . .*

Wednesday morning we got up very early. We watched the sun rise to see if it came up darker than normal. It seemed just as bright as before.

"The end is coming today," Wilbur Lee reassured us. "We must keep watching the sun."

Watch the sun we did. In fact, we did hardly anything else. As the day wore on without any apparent change in brightness, Wilbur Lee became quite agitated and paced the floor. By evening it was apparent that the sun was as bright as any other day.

"Why didn't the sun go dark?" Wilbur Lee was furious. "You said the end would come today. You lied to me!" he accused the Father.

He's accusing the Father of lying? I was shocked.

"No, I did not lie to you, the sun *is* losing its shine," Wilbur Lee repeated the answer as it came to him. "Tomorrow it will be darker than today. Every day it will lose more of its shine until I come."

The next morning the four of us went to the hardware store and Wilbur Lee purchased several dark welding lenses. "We can use these to watch the sun more closely. We will watch it closely every day."

At the next meeting, he announced, "You must buy welding lenses and really watch the sun closely. I can tell the sun is darkening. It is not shining as hot through the windows of my house. I can tell a difference already."

The following days were spent diligently studying the sun.

By the next meeting, the group was animated. "Yes, we can see it darkening. It looks more dark red. It feels cooler at our houses too," some of the members asserted. The group buzzed with excitement all evening.

We left for home with renewed anticipation. The bus would soon come and take us to paradise.

Chapter 19

The Spirit of the Engine

The weather was cold and the snow was blowing. It was February 1992. The four of us were driving south on US 131 after spending several days in Holland. The car stereo was playing some classical music Wilbur Lee had purchased. The trunk held various other items we had bought. My mind was not on the music; instead, I was absorbed in my own thoughts. The snow pelting against the window and the slushy road conditions seemed to match my somber mood.

Lately it seemed we were on the road at least two to three days a week, and sometimes more. Yesterday, after eating at a steakhouse, we had returned to our motel and watched a movie. I couldn't help but feel guilty. *How can we spend all this money so freely? I wonder if the group realizes that the money they handed over to Wilbur Lee is being used for this.*

I couldn't understand my feelings. It hurt to try to

analyze my thoughts. Finally, I dozed off into a troubled sleep.

A honking horn jerked me awake. We'd been about to pass a semi when he unexpectedly turned in front of us. Mary Alice hit the brakes and put us into a spin. We slid sideways into the median, and as the car slid down the embankment, it rolled onto its top.

Mary Alice quickly shut off the engine and asked, "Is everybody all right?"

I'm not hurting anywhere, I thought, a bit disoriented from sleep and from my awkward position. "Yes," I answered.

Calvin and I had started to untangle ourselves when Mary Alice announced, "I can't open my door."

"I can open mine," Wilbur Lee said as he pushed on his door.

I heard a strong voice booming, "Is everybody all right? Is anybody hurt?" A burly man helped the rest of us out of the car.

"There's a wrecker up ahead. I'll go see if he can help us out," Wilbur Lee said, pointing to a wrecker that was pulling another car out of a ditch.

Wilbur Lee returned and informed us, "The wrecker man called in and said they will send another truck out in a few minutes to haul the car in to the garage."

It was not long until the wrecker came and picked the car up, and we all headed to the garage. Thankfully, because of the soft snow, nothing major was wrong but a cracked windshield and a dent on top. They blew the gravel out of the brakes and sent us on our way. *Maybe this happened because of my doubts,* I thought guiltily. *I must not let anyone know I feel this way.*

Later that evening Wilbur Lee paced the floor with a slight limp. "Why, Father, did this accident happen? You must have a reason for it," he pleaded. He stopped, turned his face toward the ceiling, and closed his eyes. His lips were moving.

"Oh, Father," he said at last, "you mean to tell me that it is the engine?" He held out his hand and checked his finger pressure.

"Yes, Father, it's the engine. It is the spirit in the engine. Oh, Father, now I understand."

He continued relaying what the Father brought to his mind. "The reason the sun has not fully darkened yet is because I want to show mercy to the whole world. I charge you, Wilbur Lee, to take this message of my gospel to the whole world.

"This is the message you must share. You are my prophet. I have conveyed to you the truth. The sun will go dark, and then the end of the world will come.

"But, Father, how will the people believe this?

"All engines have spirits. They are under my control. At my command, they will cease to run. Your engine will be the only one that runs. By this seal, the world will know you are my chosen prophet. At that hour you will go forth and deliver this message. Those who will believe my gospel and accept you as my chosen prophet will inherit the earth with you. Those who reject my gospel and you as my prophet will be cast into everlasting torment in utter darkness with Lucifer and his demons."

Mary Alice and Calvin were excited about this new revelation, but I remained silent. My thoughts were busy, and questions began to push into my consciousness—questions I knew should never be asked. *What about the rapture? What about the bus? Why the changing dates?* Some things were not adding up. But these thoughts were promptly wrestled into obedience.

* * *

The car sputtered and the engine stopped. Mary Alice cranked the wheel and steered us into the driveway of a vacant lot. The four of us had been enjoying a little road trip. Now we fell dead quiet.

I looked at Wilbur Lee and saw that he was a bit distressed. *Now what?* I wondered.

"Oliver, what is wrong? Why did you shut down?" he questioned urgently.

Oliver? I thought, my stomach knotting. *Oh, yes, he said this engine's spirit is named Oliver.*

"Oliver! Oliver! What is wrong here?" Wilbur Lee sounded disturbed. Finally he lapsed into silence.

We waited. There was still no answer.

Two hours rolled by while Wilbur Lee talked with Oliver and the Father. We still hadn't opened the hood.

Mary Alice and Calvin waited patiently, dozing off at times. I couldn't hold still, so I climbed out to enjoy the beautiful spring day. *How long are we going to sit here?* I wondered impatiently. *Why doesn't he just ask for help?* Cars whizzed past us. *I wonder what they are thinking. Four adults have been sitting here for four hours! This is sick!* I crawled back into the car. I noticed how free and independent other people seemed to be. *I'm sure if their engines shut down, they'd just call a garage for help. Why can't we?*

"We are still stranded here because the Father is showing us how it will be on that day when all the engines shut down," Wilbur Lee explained patiently.

All we need to do is tow it into town, I stormed to myself. *This engine is made up of steel and wires and runs on fuel. It is not any different from any other engine around here. It's probably not getting its fuel or something simple.* I had never been able to make myself believe that engines had spirits. I was feeling irked at Wilbur Lee, and his theories had begun to disgust me.

"This lesson is so serious that Oliver won't start the engine until we get it towed to a garage," Wilbur Lee explained. He sent Calvin to a house just down the road to call a tow truck.

The mechanic at the garage checked it out. "It's just a minor problem with the fuel pump," he reported shortly.

I was disgusted. *We wasted four hours sitting there when we probably could have fixed it ourselves!* I thought.

Wilbur Lee must have sensed my impatience. "Remember how I've told you many times that we must let the Spirit do our reasoning. Don't reason for yourself. The Father has His purposes in all He does. Just think like a twelve-year-old. Be old enough to follow but young enough not to question why."

I bowed my head, ashamed of my rebellious thoughts. I remembered what all Wilbur Lee was sacrificing for us. He was constantly intervening for us in the spirit world. I would probably have been in outer darkness a long time already had it not been for him. Once again, I pushed down my doubts, and like a twelve-year-old, I followed my leader.

Chapter 20

From Bad to Worse

"We can read in Genesis that God cursed the earth." Wilbur Lee started in with one of his teachings as we sat together in one of our twice-a-week meetings. "The Spirit revealed to me that's why I wasn't allowed to plant gardens in previous years and again this spring. If any of you want to raise vegetables, you will need to do it in greenhouses from now on." He went on to explain how we should make our greenhouses. We were to buy all our soil, because the soil on the ground was cursed.

That spring the group got busy building greenhouses. Gardens were seeded into grass again. The food that couldn't be raised in the greenhouses was bought from stores. Canning was not looked on as a necessity, because food could be raised in the greenhouse year-round.

Wilbur Lee never did get his greenhouse built.

One summer evening after a meeting at Dad's place, I asked Toby, "How's your greenhouse doing?"

"Pretty good," he said. "Want to go see it?"

"Sure," I replied. We crossed the lawn toward the greenhouse. "Do you enjoy working in the greenhouse?" I asked, inspecting the plants with interest.

"Not really. I wish I were a disciple; then I could have an easier life." Toby's voice sounded almost bitter.

"What do you mean?" I asked.

"Well, it's hard for our family to survive on a hundred and fifty dollars a week. That's all Wilbur Lee gives us. He says that's enough to survive until the Father comes. By the time we buy the potting soil and other necessities, there isn't much left. Often we eat just one meal a day. Sometimes I just get so hungry! But I guess this helps me focus on paradise." Toby had his voice under control again.

"Remember, he told us tonight that we can get jobs as soon as the Father lets us," I said, hoping to lift his spirits. I felt sorry for him, yet I did not dare show it, lest he detect that I had my doubts too.

"I know. That's what he told us last week and the week before that." Toby shook his head, quickly adding, "I shouldn't feel this way. Wilbur Lee has done so much for us; we can do without some things so he can take the lessons the Father wants to give him."

"Keep looking forward to paradise. It will be worth it all once we get there," I encouraged him.

* * *

Months passed. We frequently took overnight road trips. We stayed in motels a lot. We watched television a lot, both at home and at the motels. Wilbur Lee often went into the bathroom to meditate while Mary Alice, Calvin, and I watched sitcoms. I was fascinated by the independence I saw in the characters on the shows. *I wonder how it feels to be that free. Is everybody outside of our group free to make his own decisions? I am sure the Amish are not free, not with all their senseless rules and traditions.*

After a day of traveling, we were relaxing in a motel, all watching television. As I flipped through the channels, I came across a romantic scene. We watched it for about ten minutes. I felt guilty at the feelings that stirred within me. *I am not supposed to feel attracted to women. What is wrong with me?* I stole a glance at Wilbur Lee and saw his disinterested expression. He was clearly unaffected by the scene.

That night after everyone was in bed, I struggled with my feelings. *Am I perverted to long to love a woman? I know Wilbur Lee warns against these feelings, but I can't help it. What is wrong with me?* Guilt pressed on my heart.

The next morning Wilbur Lee wanted to take a little walk before leaving for home. I decided to join him. I still felt very confused.

We were walking along in silence when I had a sudden desire to share my struggle with him. I was sure he had answers for me. "I feel myself attracted to women, especially when watching television. I am not sure what is happening to me." There, it was out.

Wilbur Lee looked surprised. "Really! I can't believe you are attracted to women. They are designed by Lucifer. How can you find them attractive?" he sneered. "Lucifer is giving you these thoughts. You must spend more time with the Spirit."

"I appreciate your advice. I will try to be more faithful to the Father and communicate with the Spirit," I responded, feeling very discouraged.

* * *

It was a chilly day in March, and we were spending the forenoon cleaning up the yard. I was nineteen, and I increasingly felt that something was amiss. My discouragement had progressed to depression. As I worked, I replayed Wilbur Lee's teachings in my mind.

I remembered one afternoon Wilbur Lee had taught us more revelations he had recently received from the Father. We were sitting in a semicircle, giving him our full attention. Wilbur Lee was pacing in front of us as he usually did when he was about to share important new revelations.

"Did you ever think about how a God of love could kill His own Son? He told Abraham to kill his own son. The Bible says God is a God of fire-flamed eyes and a consuming fire. Does that sound like a loving God to you? Did you know that Jesus Christ never rose from the dead? That is a lie! People believe in a dead Savior! Who else but Lucifer would kill his own son? Heaven is a lie from Lucifer. He gives people visions of heaven, causing them to believe that heaven is real. It is all a lie."

I recalled another time when Wilbur Lee had said Jesus never came in a bodily form.

But if Jesus never came in bodily form, how could God as Lucifer kill Him? My thoughts were in turmoil.

Various people had approached us quoting the verse, "But though we, or an angel from heaven, preach any other gospel unto you than that which we have preached unto you, let him be accursed." They meant that we should not listen to Wilbur Lee. But Wilbur Lee said, "I have another gospel. Curses come from Lucifer, so he put that verse in the Bible."

How can I know for sure? I wondered.

I remembered the time Wilbur Lee had said, "Jesus is Satan, Lucifer's son." Shortly after that a well-meaning neighbor had asked, "Do you believe Jesus is God's Son?"

I had replied, "Yes, I do," all the while thinking that couldn't be right, as we were being taught that Jesus was Lucifer's son.

Suppose Wilbur Lee is deceived? What if he is wrong? But what if he is right? How can I know? I can't go to my Amish family members. I don't want to be Amish.

I pushed these thoughts down to the innermost part of my heart.

The next evening, after another day of Spirit-led traveling, we settled in the living room as Wilbur Lee again received revelations from the Father. He was agitated as he turned toward the three of us and relayed the revelation. "You are lost! You are damned in hell forever. You have no hope. Hell is your lot forever. You will be in torment and horrible anguish and agony, writhing in extreme pain. The one side of you will be frozen solid and the other half will be sizzling hot."

He swore. His face was crimson and sweat dripped from his forehead.

"You doubt my teachings. You desire a woman instead of me. You do not perform reliably."

We were shocked. Our faces turned ashen.

Does he actually know my thoughts? I wondered fearfully.

"Is there really no hope?" I asked in a weak, quivering voice.

"No. The Father told me there is no place for you in paradise. There is a place prepared for you in hell. Lucifer cannot wait to get hold of your soul and cast you into outer darkness where there will be fire and brimstone and gnashing of teeth, screaming with no rest forever and ever."

We all broke down and wept bitterly, as only those who are damned can.

Wilbur Lee sat down heavily on his chair. I stumbled blindly to him, fell down at his knees, and desperately pleaded, "Please, please, is there no way you can help us? Somehow, please!"

At this, he broke down and wept.

Silence followed. The only sound was our pitiful weeping as we tried to come to grips with the utter lost condition of our souls.

Wilbur Lee's tear-filled gaze turned upward. "Oh, Father, I intervene desperately for these lost souls. Can you please make a way for them? Somehow, oh, Father, somehow. You know how I have always obeyed you and tried so hard to impart all your teachings to my followers in a most faithful manner."

Immediately he received the Father's answer. His face lighted as he relayed the message he had just received to us. "Because of your perfect obedience to me and your intervention on behalf of your disciples, I will show mercy. If they accept my teachings without doubting, they can have life in paradise."

Incredible relief flooded my being. I cried, "Oh, thank you, Wilbur Lee, thank you. How can I thank you enough?"

The following days, even as I reveled in my newfound

deliverance from damnation, somehow deep down within me I wondered if Wilbur Lee had been playing with our minds.

One evening we were discussing our damnation when Wilbur Lee turned to us and said, "The lesson the Father wished to teach you was that you might vividly feel how lost you would be without me as your leader."

Ah! So we really were not lost. He was *just playing with our minds.* I kept this thought to myself. Now I knew.

A few weeks later I was mowing the yard for the first time that season. My mind was busy. *What about Wilbur Lee's claim that the earth is only six hundred years old? That does not even make sense.* I started calculating. According to my calculations, if that were true, there could not be five billion people on earth.

I finished mowing the yard and needed to water the flowers. I walked up to the house and grabbed the hose. I went to hook it up and realized I had the wrong end. *Oh, I need the female end,* I thought. Then it hit me. *Even hoses are male and female.* I stopped and analyzed this thought. *Why, even the insects, the birds, the animals, the plants—yes, even the plants—have two genders. And here Wilbur Lee is claiming that females were not intended to be. They came from Lucifer. No way! He is wrong! The whole creation is male and female. I see it all over. Humans cannot be any different. This is the right design. It is supposed to be this way.*

I walked toward the house, my mind full. But I knew I needed to keep this to myself.

Chapter 21

A Taste of Freedom

It was a warm evening in June, and I lay in bed alone. I knew Wilbur Lee would join me soon. My mind was tired from trying to decide who was right. My thoughts replayed the events of the evening before. I pictured again in my mind how I had sat on the step of the old barn and how God had vividly shown me that He loved me by sending those three meteorites streaking through the night sky. *Now I know for sure that there is a loving God.* I reveled in this feeling of fresh hope. *But what should I do now? I know I have to leave. But then what?*

I reviewed my carefully laid plans. Earlier in the afternoon, I had crept into Mary Alice's bedroom and found her purse. There was plenty of cash in there. *This is my parents' money,* I had thought defensively, pulling out three hundred dollars. *I will pay them back someday,* I told myself. *I will sneak out of the house and be gone before dawn. I will hitchhike to Holland. There are many churches there. Surely one of them has the answers.*

But what if Wilbur Lee is right? I could be damned forever in hellfire. Doubts still plagued me. I longed for freedom. So I prayed, *Father, please show me somehow that this is the right thing to do.* It seemed strange to be praying to a different Father than Wilbur Lee's father.

I slowly relaxed and dozed off. Suddenly, as in a vision, I saw Jesus standing before me. I was kneeling in front of Him. I sensed Satan behind me. He had a long knife raised, ready to strike. I was terrified. As I looked pleadingly to Jesus, I realized Satan had to go. Jesus had power over Satan. Now I was alone with Jesus. "What shall I do?" I pleaded.

"Do what I say," He instructed.

I was back in bed, wide-awake. *Jesus is my Savior,* I realized. *But I wish He had told me what to do. Now I know He is not dead.* I fell asleep.

Suddenly I woke up. Sunlight was streaming in the window. My heart jumped into my throat. *What time is it?* I had planned to leave by three o'clock. I looked to my right. Wilbur Lee was sound asleep beside me. Calvin was sleeping in the twin bed on the other side of the room.

I slid out of bed and slipped into my clothes. My companions never stirred. I crept down the basement stairs, pulling a paper out of my pocket. On it was a sketch I had drawn several days before showing a boy standing at a crossroad with a signpost. On the signpost were many different arrows with various destinations listed. It described my confused state of mind. I had purposely drawn this to use as my departure note. I found a pen and scribbled,

I am leaving. Do not look for me. Wil.

I hurried to open a box I had located a few days prior and snatched out my social security card. I crept up the steps and stole into the entryway, where I paused and slowly let out my breath. I had not realized I was holding it. I softly opened the door, stepped out, and closed it silently. I walked across the lawn, stepped onto US Highway 20, and headed west. I was out.

I have to keep moving, I thought. I stuck out my thumb. Almost immediately, a car slowed and stopped. "Do you need a ride?" asked a friendly Mennonite driver.

"Sure do," I responded gratefully. I jumped in the car and rode away from my old life.

"Where are you going?" my friendly driver asked.

"North of Middlebury," I answered.

He dropped me off at Middlebury, and I resumed my hike. I had decided to go to Kalamazoo, Michigan, and catch a bus on to Holland. I was barely out of town when I removed my despised suspenders and threw them into the ditch. I felt liberated! *I want to get out of these Amish clothes as quick as I can,* I thought.

This feels great. I will never go back! I don't even feel condemned. In fact, I reasoned, *if I go to hell for leaving Wilbur Lee, then I'll meet him there. That was nothing less than a cult!*

After arriving in Michigan, I decided to buy some clothes. I entered a Tractor Supply store and searched the clothing section. I found a western-style shirt and a pair of jeans and headed for the fitting room. I tore off my Amish clothes and happily slipped into my new ones. I viewed my reflection and was pleased with what I saw, except for my plain haircut. I ripped the tags off my new clothes, bundled up my old ones, and headed for the checkout. I tossed the tags on the counter. The cashier looked at me with a comical expression. She politely did not question me about my clothes and took the money I offered. I was soon on my way.

I arrived in Holland about 3:30 in the afternoon and checked in at a Comfort Inn. The receptionist asked me for a driver's license, but of course I did not have one, so I showed her my social security card.

Once in my room I sat on a chair and tried to collect my thoughts. I decided to try to locate a farmer who would employ me and provide room and board. I picked up the complimentary newspaper from the nightstand and flipped through to the Help Wanted section.

I found several ads that seemed likely. I picked up the phone and dialed the first number. The phone rang twice before a deep voice answered, "Hello."

"Hello. This is Wil Hochstetler," I replied. "I saw your help wanted ad in the paper, and I am looking for work."

"Do you have any experience with farm machinery?"

"Well, yes. I've done some work with a tractor," I responded vaguely.

"Where do you live?"

Uh-oh, I thought. "Well, I am sort of between addresses right now," I admitted.

There was a long, awkward pause.

"You see, I need a place to board and work, so I thought a farm would suit well." I broke the silence.

"I am sorry, but I don't have a place to board, so I don't believe this will work out," he stated apologetically.

My heart sank. "Okay. Bye," I finished as I hung up.

I tried three other help wanted ads with no better success.

Now what? I wondered, discouraged.

The next morning I walked to the employment agency. I opened the door and walked in, showing more confidence than I actually felt.

"Good morning," greeted the receptionist. "How can I help you?"

"I am looking for employment, and I thought you might be able to help me out."

"Please fill out this form," she directed as she pushed a long form attached to a clipboard my way.

I filled it out as best I could and handed it back.

"Oh," she said, raising her eyebrows, "you forgot to fill in your address."

"Well, uh, actually I am just staying at a motel right now and am in the area looking for a job. I am also looking for a place to stay."

"Did you check at the city mission? I can direct you there if you wish," she suggested kindly. "It's a place you can stay rent-free until you find a job."

"Thank you. I think I will."

I walked to the city mission later that afternoon. A tall gentleman stepped out of an office and approached me.

"How are you?" he asked kindly.

"I am well, thanks," I responded.

"How can I help you?" he resumed.

"I am looking for a place to stay, and I heard you help folks like me," I said hopefully.

After a few more questions, he went over a list of rules.

One of them was that I would search for a job every day. I complied gladly and faithfully went job shopping.

A pastor worked at the mission. I confided in him about Wilbur Lee and running away. He seemed understanding of my plight. His impression was that I came from a decent background and was clean because I never did drugs. Unfortunately, he never questioned deeply. But he gave me a Bible, which I treasured greatly. I had never had my own Bible.

One evening the pastor invited me out for dinner. We were driving along, enjoying ourselves and visiting, and I confided some of my struggles. "When I was involved with the cult, the power and control the leader had over us was awful. Even now I am still very confused."

"I would encourage you to read the last part of Romans chapter one where it talks about the state of man without God," he said.

His words were scarcely out of his mouth when the car sputtered and went silent. We coasted to a stop and looked at each other. I froze. *Maybe the spirit of the engine heard us talking. Is Wilbur Lee right after all? This must be the end. I am going to be lost!*

He looked over to me and confidently said, "Don't worry. This thing will start in a few minutes."

Other cars were not stopping, so this could not be the end. He tried the ignition several times, and finally it started up. Relief flooded over me.

Upon returning, I opened my Bible to Romans chapter one. I was astonished at how accurately it described my situation.

One evening, after I had spent a week at the mission, a

staff member insisted that I call home to report that I was okay.

"I really don't want to do that," I stalled.

"I know, but you must, because it really is not fair to your parents. They must wonder if you are all right," he persisted.

I knew he was right. Since we'd left the Amish church, my parents had gotten a phone. *I guess it will probably be safe, because I'm sure they don't want me back anyway*, I decided. So I called home.

Mom answered the phone. "Hello."

"Hello, this is Wil."

"Oh, it's you, Wil." She sounded relieved.

"I just wanted to let you know that I am okay, but I've made my decision to leave the group. I'm not coming home," I said lightly.

"But we want you to come home," she begged. "Here, let Peter talk with you. He's here right now."

"Hello, Wil." He sounded serious.

"Hi, Peter."

"Where are you?"

"I'm in Holland at the city mission."

"Where in Holland is that?"

I refused to answer.

"Wil, you must come home," he begged.

"I made up my mind not to return," I stated with finality.

His voice began to quiver. "But you must. Wilbur Lee said that if you do not come home we will all be eternally lost."

I heard a voice cry in the background, "He must, he just

must come home!" I heard loud sobbing and crying as my decision reached my family members.

I hung up. The staff member returned. "Did you call?"

"Yes, but they will be lost forever!" I cried to him.

"What do you mean? Who will be lost forever?"

"My family, the group, all of them!" I was sobbing. I couldn't control my emotions anymore. "I was part of a cult," I tried to explain. I could not put my condition into words.

The staff member kindly questioned me as I tried to explain my unusual circumstances. It seemed I couldn't get the seriousness through to him.

Several hours later, a staff member announced that someone was there to see me.

My heart froze. *Who could be here?*

"Do you want me to go with you?" he offered.

"No, I'll go alone. I'm okay." I tried to sound confident.

I entered the waiting room and found Wilbur Lee, Calvin, and Mary Alice waiting for me. My heart sank.

Wilbur Lee was smiling serenely. "How are you, Wil?" he asked smoothly. He looked me over. "Wil, you look really good. I like your haircut." I had gotten a short haircut at the mission. My new clothes also changed my appearance.

"I'm fine," I said as I sat down stiffly. "I want you to know that I now believe in Jesus as my Savior." I expected a heated reaction.

Wilbur Lee smiled broadly. "That's okay, Wil. If that's what you want to believe, that is fine." He sounded so gracious. "I am not like the Amish. If you want to go your own way, I will help you get started."

"Really?" I was surprised at the offer. I felt encouraged. Maybe if he would help me get started I wouldn't have to live in this homeless shelter.

"If you come home with us, I will help you get started. The four of us will go on a long trip out West together. I have wanted to do this for a long time already."

My mind was spinning.

"Wouldn't you enjoy a trip like that?"

"Yes," I answered cautiously.

"Won't you come back with us so you don't have to remain homeless?" he asked enticingly.

"Well," I said slowly, "I will if you help me get started." I took his bait.

"I'll help you get started if you promise not to run off without telling me first. If you are man enough to make your own decisions, then you should be man enough to tell me when you're leaving."

I nodded numbly. I felt myself being drawn back under his power. I felt helpless to resist.

I gathered my clothes and meekly followed them out the door, stepping out into the dark night toward the waiting car. Mary Alice started the car and drove us to the Comfort Inn, where we checked in. I carried my meager belongings and followed the three up the stairs and down the hall. Wilbur Lee opened the door and we all filed in and set our luggage on the bed.

Wilbur Lee turned to me and asked, "May I see your Bible?"

Slowly I handed it over to him. "One of the staff at the mission gave it to me," I said, trying to convey how much it meant to me.

"I will take care of this for you," he said as he set it up on the shelf.

I suddenly regretted my promise not to leave again without telling him. I was back in. My heart sank as a wave of despair engulfed me.

Chapter 22

Almost Persuaded

"Wil, Wil!" I woke with a start. Wilbur Lee was shaking my shoulders. It was early the next morning.

"What?" I exclaimed in alarm.

"I thought you had stopped breathing!"

"Well, I am still here." I grinned slightly.

"I thought Lucifer took your life," he explained. "What you did was very serious. Running away from the Father has grave consequences."

I did not respond. His ranting was all too familiar.

As we got ready to leave, he said, "I will keep your clothes in this garbage bag until you go on your own."

I grimaced as I pulled on my old broadfall pants. *Oh, well, maybe he'll give me back my Bible. Then at least I'll have one thing to remind me of my new life,* I comforted myself.

On our way to the car, I saw Wilbur Lee heading for the garbage dumpster.

I wonder what he wants over there, I thought.

As he lifted the lid, I saw it. He had my Bible! He discreetly slipped it inside.

My heart dropped. I felt doomed.

We quietly climbed into Mary Alice's car and headed for home, Wilbur Lee in the driver's seat.

"Wil, why did you decide to leave?" he asked softly.

I related the experiences I had with God and ended by reemphasizing that I had Jesus as my Savior now.

"I have seen so much hypocrisy," Wilbur Lee sneered. "Christians are no better than the world. Take Halloween, for example. That is actually the devil's night, and the Amish youth celebrate it. Why would good Christians do something like that? Is that consistent? No, of course not!"

I stayed firm. I knew my experience was real. "Jesus Christ is my Savior," I said with conviction.

He lifted both arms and slammed his fists on the steering wheel. "Look at everything I've done for you, and now you do this to me!" He was livid.

This time I remained silent.

The rest of the trip was quiet.

Within two weeks we headed out West. We toured many states and various state parks. We were gone for five weeks. Wilbur Lee spent a lot of time talking to me, trying to persuade me to believe in him again.

I remained passive. I didn't challenge him; neither did I support his teachings. I kept telling myself, "As soon as I get back, I am getting out." The new world he was exposing me to beckoned me.

When we returned, I asked Wilbur Lee, "How soon are you going to help me get started on my own?"

"The Father has revealed that it is His will that all of us move to Holland. When we get up there, I will help you get started," he reassured me. I was disheartened, but I felt powerless to resist this new development.

If only I could get help somewhere, I thought. *I don't want to be Amish, so I can't go to my family. I can't trust anybody else. I'll just have to stick this out until we can go. Surely we'll go soon.*

I was wrong. Several weeks later, he came up with another idea. "Let's go on an eastern trip." He sounded enthusiastic.

I had enjoyed the sights and scenery of the previous trip, so I didn't object to this. *At least I can see the world at someone else's expense,* I thought.

This time we toured the New England states. Again we were gone for five weeks. Again he spent a lot of time indoctrinating me. Though I didn't challenge him, I felt frustrated with his endless delays. I determined to hold him to his promise when we got back.

As soon as we got home, I confronted Wilbur Lee. "How soon are we moving to Holland?"

"We will go when the Father tells us to. I really want to, it's just that the Father hasn't given us permission to go yet," he said.

The weeks kept passing. The leaves started to turn, yet Wilbur Lee kept coming up with more excuses not to move. One day I confronted him again. "When are we going to move to Holland?"

"Oh, it's fall now, and we don't want to move when it's cold," he stalled. "It says in the Bible that we should pray that our flight will not be in the winter."

"But you told me you would help me get started, and I will hold you to it," I argued. By then I was extremely angry. *I hate this man,* I seethed.

Winter dragged on, and I kept reminding him of his promise. He seemed indifferent to me. Clearly, begging didn't work. Meanwhile, Calvin and I learned how to drive. We drove around the community without a license.

Finally, when March rolled around, we went to Holland, searching for apartments. Surprisingly, we found one on the first trip. Within two weeks the four of us had packed our belongings, rented a U-haul, and moved to Holland. We rented two apartments next to each other with two bedrooms each. Calvin and I slept in one apartment and Wilbur Lee and Mary Alice slept in the other. Despite our separation, I still did not feel liberated. He lived right there and watched me closely.

As soon as we were settled in, I told Wilbur Lee, "I am going to get a job."

"The only requirement is that you help pay the rent for the apartments," he said. I was relieved.

I quickly found a job selling fire extinguishers. The company was set up using multi-level marketing. They, of course, promised I would make big money.

I also decided to attend church services. Every Sunday I joined the worshipers at the local Wesleyan church. I enjoyed the fellowship immensely. They had a nice youth group, and I enjoyed going along on the youth outings.

But Wilbur Lee's teachings and the inconsistencies I saw in the churches continued to confuse me. In my desire to have a good time, I decided to try to forget God and all religion. I felt a huge emptiness within me. I desperately wanted to prove to Wilbur Lee that I could succeed without him.

Unfortunately, I did not make big money selling fire extinguishers. But I was able to work my way up to an office manager position, which gave me the privilege of choosing a city in which to set up my own sales office.

A sales office became available in Indianapolis, and I took the opportunity. So in September of 1993 I moved down to Indianapolis to pursue my career.

Chapter 23

Reunited

In Indianapolis I could do as I pleased. There was a huge emptiness in my heart, and I attempted to fill it with good times and social activities. I was disillusioned with religion, but though I didn't realize it, God was patiently working on my heart.

"There is nothing to religion. It is all one big confusion. One person says it is like this. Another says it is like that," I argued to my friend Mike one day.

"Wil," he said, "if you had experienced what I did in my life, you would not say that."

"You only believe what you have been taught." I tried again. "If you had been taught that blue is pink, you would call it that."

He didn't argue, but went on to relate his experience. "One day my little girl walked out on thin ice—thinner than I could walk on. She was so terrified that she could not move when I called her. I just prayed to God to save her from breaking through and drowning. I called her again, and she relaxed and immediately walked back to me. I know God is real because He heard and answered my prayer."

In December I took a week off for Christmas vacation and decided to go up north to visit my Amish family members, whom I had not seen for quite a few years. I decided I would stop and see my brother David first. I knew he used to work at Hochstetler Siding and live next door. I walked up the sidewalk leading to the house and knocked. A man came to the door and greeted me with a friendly, "Hello, can I help you?"

I was surprised to see a strange face and asked, "Does David live here?"

"No, not anymore," he replied, "but he works at the lumberyard next door."

"Thanks. I'll drive over and check there," I said as I turned to leave.

I walked into the store and approached the woman behind the counter. "I am looking for David."

"Oh, Dave? He's in his office. I'll go get him."

A moment later, David walked toward me. "Can I help you?" he offered courteously.

"Well, don't you know me?" I asked in surprise.

His expression changed. A look of recognition flashed across his face. It seemed like he wanted to say my name, but he did not trust his intuition. "No," he finally admitted.

"Well, I'm your brother."

He gasped in surprise. "Wil!" he exclaimed, grabbing my outstretched hand.

He led me back to his office. "How are you doing?

What brings you here? I haven't seen you in years! My, how you have grown!"

"I'm sure I've changed a lot," I laughed.

"Yes, your mustache fooled me, I guess," he chuckled.

David's boss let him off for the rest of the day. We went to his home for lunch and reminisced about bygone days.

"I have to tell you what happened to me one day," he said. "Apparently, Toby needed to haul some garbage with the wagon and a team of horses. He had to drive by our new place, where Mary and I have lived since we married. It had been a long time since I had seen the family that's with the group, and I was lonely for you all. I saw Toby coming up the road and rushed out to meet him. The driveway was quite long, but I still made it nearly to the road. 'Toby, Toby!' I shouted, but Toby stared straight ahead, never acknowledging me. I just leaned on the board fence and sobbed."

"I-yi-yi," I sympathized. "I know it seems really strange, but we were so brainwashed that it just seemed like the right thing to do."

Around four o'clock that afternoon I said, "I want to visit our brother Dan yet."

"I wonder if he will recognize you," David said.

"I won't say who I am when I meet him," I chuckled.

I found Dan in the barn milking the cows. I walked up to him.

"Hello," he said.

"Hello," I responded. "Don't you know me?"

"Are you neighbor Tom Smith's son?" he asked.

"No, I'm your brother," I corrected him.

He stared at me in disbelief. "Wil!" he exclaimed. "It's

good to see you!"

"Same here," I responded happily.

"How long has it been?" Dan asked.

"I think it's been at least seven years since I've seen any of my Amish family. I visited David this afternoon, and he didn't recognize me either," I chuckled.

"Did David tell you we are gathering at Elmer's place for Christmas tomorrow?" he asked.

"Yes, he did, and I'm planning to come too. Is it all right if I stay here for the night?" I inquired.

"Certainly. I'll finish my chores and we'll head inside," he invited.

The next morning I drove to my brother Elmer's house. I walked up to the front door and knocked. Elmer's wife Esther opened the door.

"Hello," I said. "Do you remember me?"

"No," she said. "Are you selling something?"

Before I had a chance to answer, Elmer walked up behind her. He looked a bit stern.

"Hello," I addressed him. "Do you remember me?" I saw David smiling in the background.

"No. Should I?" he asked.

"Yes. I'm your brother," I said.

"Wil!" He shook my hand and welcomed me into the house.

Soon my brother Dan and his family arrived, and we had a wonderful time together. Before I left, David informed me, "There will be another family gathering at the end of January. Alva and Elnora plan to be here. You would be most welcome to join us again."

"I will certainly plan to be here," I responded, already

looking forward to it.

* * *

In January I arrived at my brother David's house for the family gathering. Alva and Elnora walked out to my car to meet me. I stepped out, clasped my older brother's outstretched hand, and shook it warmly.

"Wil! It's good to see you again!" Alva said. "It has been a long time."

"It's so good to see you too," I returned.

Later in the day, Alva and I talked about my experiences with the group and out on my own.

"Alva, I am so discouraged. Nothing is really working out for me. I am almost out of money, and my jobs don't seem to pan out very well." It felt good to share my struggles with someone I could trust.

"We have been praying for you, and our hearts go out to you," Alva said warmly. "Why don't you come live with us? We've moved to Evart, Michigan. I would see that you get a good job, and you could board with us for as long as you like."

"I don't want to join the Amish," I said, shaking my head.

"Why don't you just come anyway? You can decide later what you want to do. We will not pressure you into joining our church. We just want to help you any way we can," Alva offered graciously.

"I appreciate your offer, and I will think about it," I stalled.

Later that night I struggled with Alva's offer. Wilbur Lee had painted a negative picture of the Amish. What did

I really believe about them?

Lord, what should I do? I prayed. *Should I move in with Alva, or should I forget about it? How can I know what is best?* Toward morning, I finally leaned toward trying it. What did I really have to lose?

After breakfast I told David that I had decided to go live with Alva and Elnora in Evart.

"Good, I'm glad," he encouraged me.

That afternoon I returned to Indianapolis to pack my bags.

Chapter 24

New Beginnings

I turned into Alva and Elnora's driveway with apprehension. What would my life in Evart be like?

Elnora welcomed me warmly. I carried my luggage in and got everything situated in my room. Soon Alva came home from work for lunch. After he welcomed me and showed me around the place, we went inside to eat.

Throughout the next several days, Alva and I had many long discussions about my life with Wilbur Lee. Freely sharing my experiences allowed me to view them from a completely different perspective. Many times I was embarrassed to relate what our group had believed.

On Sunday, church services were held at Alva's house. I sat in rapt attention as the ministers expounded God's Word. I felt like a dry sponge soaking up the living water of truth.

"Jesus was here as a human being, yet He was without

sin," the minister preached. "His purpose was to bring hope to lost mankind. He is the great healer of our souls. One of his missions on earth was to bring physical healing. This was God's way to get people to believe Him. He healed a number of lepers. Leprosy was a terminal illness, yet He healed them every time."

Wilbur Lee never healed anyone. He could not even heal Maribeth's cancer, I reasoned. Suddenly my vision of Jesus came to my mind. I hadn't thought about it for months. *Maybe Jesus is the Son of God after all. The minister certainly seems confident that what he is preaching is the truth. He isn't spending any time knocking other churches; he is simply presenting the Bible.*

"The Bible is absolutely true," the minister continued. "How do we know it is true? First of all because of the difference it makes in our lives when we believe its truths and live them. Jesus tells us in His Word what we are to do."

My mind flashed back to my vision. *Oh, so that's what Jesus meant when He told me, "Do as I say." Perhaps if I had searched the Bible and believed everything it said, things would have turned out differently. My life sure is a mess right now. I need to find the truth.*

After church the bishop walked up to me. "So you are Wil, Alva's brother?"

"Yes, I am."

"My name is Omer Miller. I'm glad to see you here. You are welcome to come to our house to visit anytime," he invited.

That evening Alva and I sat in the living room visiting.

My thoughts returned to the sermon.

"Alva, how do you know the Bible is true?" I asked.

"I simply believe it is true," he stated with confidence. "It has made all the difference in my life."

"When I left Wilbur Lee the first time, I read the first chapter of Romans. I could really identify with that."

"That is what you need to do. You have to read the Bible. The more you read it, the clearer it will become," he advised. "All the answers to our troubles are in there."

"So, you don't believe it makes one proud to read the Bible too much?" I asked.

Alva chuckled. "No, certainly not. If we read it for the right reasons, it will humble us. It shows us how sinful we are before God and how helpless we are without Him."

"Why would God kill His Son Jesus if He is a God of love?" I wondered.

"God did not kill Him. The angry people killed Him. However, God allowed Him to die because there was no other way for us humans to be saved from our sins. Ever since Adam and Eve sinned, blood was required to redeem the sinner from his condemnation. God is righteous; therefore, He cannot tolerate any sin. All of us have sinned at some time in our lives. In the Old Testament, the priest would offer an animal's blood as atonement, which worked for a time, but God wanted to cleanse us from our sins for all time. Animals were not sufficient to take away our sins.

"The only person who qualified was Jesus, because He never committed a sin. He was completely pure and innocent. He became our prophet, priest, and king. God sent Jesus down to earth in the form of a baby, and when

He grew to manhood, He endured all the temptations that we have, yet He did not commit sin. God knew that nobody is good enough by his own strength to please Him and enter heaven; therefore, God allowed the people to kill Him. However, He did not leave Him in the grave. Three days later Jesus rose from death. Now He lives at the right hand of God in heaven. If we confess our sins, believe Him with our whole heart, accept Him in our lives, and repent, or turn away from our sins, then He will give us His Holy Spirit and we can have victory over sin. Isn't that wonderful?" he asked me.

I was spellbound. I had never heard anything like this. "It seems like Wilbur Lee may have taught something like this in the beginning, but it sure didn't last long," I commented.

"When Jesus saves us from our sins, He also forgives us for all the bad things we have ever done. We don't have to live with a guilty conscience anymore. However, when we accept Jesus as our Savior, we must also accept Him as our Lord. We do what He tells us in His Word, the Bible. If we disobey Him, we become guilty again. We must confess our sins; then He will forgive us and we become clean again," Alva said.

"What if I committed the unpardonable sin of blasphemy against the Holy Ghost?" I asked.

"Well," Alva responded, "we may not know all the details about blaspheming the Holy Spirit, but there is one thing for sure, if we desire the presence of the Holy Spirit and His conviction in our life, we can rest assured that we have not turned from Him. God convicts us through the

Holy Spirit. When we choose to listen to His promptings and respond in repentance, He is faithful to forgive us.

"If you are concerned about being right with God and being filled with His righteousness, that is evidence the Holy Spirit is working in your life. If you resist Him too long, refusing to repent, and die in that state, there is no forgiveness, ever. We know one can never repent and be forgiven after death. In 1 John 1:9 it says, 'If we confess our sins, he is faithful and just to forgive us our sins, and to cleanse us from all unrighteousness.' "

Alva chuckled. "Well, according to his own teachings, Wilbur Lee must have committed the unpardonable sin."

* * *

Two evenings later I went to Bishop Omer's house to visit. He invited me inside and we made ourselves comfortable in the living room.

"So, what did you and your group believe?" he asked me.

"The group we were involved with is a cult," I began.

"It is interesting that there would be a cult consisting only of Amish," Omer said skeptically. "Why would you join a cult?"

"That is hard to explain. We were searching for meaning in life. Wilbur Lee took an interest in us and answered many of our questions," I explained. "In the beginning he taught us from the Bible, but after a while he developed his own teachings and taught us revelations he supposedly received from the Father."

"After he had lured you away from the Amish

church?" he asked.

"Yes. Once we lost faith in the things we'd been taught and those who had taught us, we were vulnerable. Now I don't even have Wilbur Lee. I guess I'm on my own."

"Do you have any plans for your future?" he asked next.

"Well, I'm sure I don't want to be Amish," I chuckled nervously.

"I see. What is your impression of the Amish?" Omer asked.

"Not very good," I responded. "Most of them are hypocrites who don't know what they believe. They allow smoking, drinking, dirty jokes, and sins like that in the church and don't do anything about it. They just live the way they do because that's the way their ancestors lived."

"Unfortunately, there are Amish churches that allow sin in the church. You will find a large variation amongst the Amish as far as what they allow and how they apply the Scriptures. But many Amish churches do not allow sin," he explained. "The Amish lifestyle does not save us. Perhaps too many Amish do believe that way, but it is not scriptural. We believe that we have eternal life by trusting Jesus for our redemption."

"So you don't think I would be saved just by joining the Amish?" I questioned.

"Certainly not," Omer answered. "We believe that Jesus Christ is the only way to eternal life."

"I've often wondered what actually is sinful about electricity or driving cars."

"True, we don't use certain modern conveniences, but

that is only for our safety, not our salvation. We believe that living a simple lifestyle brings fewer distractions to our spiritual life."

"I see. I have never heard that explanation before," I said in contemplation.

Omer continued, "It is important to understand that while these things are not evil in themselves, we as a church do see danger in them, so we make guidelines accordingly."

"I don't fully understand," I responded. "But I do know that when I decided to throw out all religion and do as I pleased, my life went to shambles."

"Did you ever have any personal encounters with God?" Omer asked next.

"Yes, actually I did," I replied. "The night before I left Wilbur Lee I experienced a vision of myself kneeling in front of Jesus." I related my experience in detail. "Am I saved by that experience?" I wondered.

"No, I would not feel that you are saved from your sins because of that experience since there was no repentance," Omer responded. "But God was certainly showing you His love and showing you a way out."

"So what must I do to be saved?" I asked.

"You must first see the sinfulness of your heart and see that you are lost without Jesus in your life. Once you realize your sinfulness, you must come to God, confess your sins, give Jesus your whole heart, and allow Him to be your Master. Jesus will cleanse your heart, forgive your sins, and fill your heart with peace. You need to trust Jesus with your whole life and be willing to follow in loving obedience. Once saved, you can rest assured you will meet Him in heaven if you remain in complete submission to Him. It is important that you realize that we are saved through His gift of grace and not by any works we have done."

I nodded soberly as I rose to leave. *This makes more sense than anything Wilbur Lee ever taught,* I thought.

I spent the next several months studying the Bible and trying to sort out the false doctrines I had been taught. It was a time of intense reflection and coming to grips with the sinfulness of my own heart. Finally, one evening as I was giving the horses their hay, I was seriously contemplating the lost condition of my heart and the great emptiness that was still not satisfied. The burden of my heart was more than I could bear, and I became desperate to find peace. I knelt beside the hay manger, spread my arms in front of me, and cried out to God.

"O God, you know how sinful I am. I am sorry for all the sins I have committed in my life. I feel so dirty. I am sorry for the times that I lied. I am sorry for hating Wilbur Lee. I am sorry for my immorality and pride. I ask you to be my Lord and Savior. Amen."

Indescribable peace enveloped my heart. Tears filled my eyes as I realized that I was delivered from Satan and his lies. Now I was a child of God. Reverently I bowed my head and whispered, "Thank you, God, for saving my soul and forgiving all my sins."

I stood up and walked out of that barn with a light heart. I was a new creature in Christ. My heart overflowed with praise and thankfulness to my Savior. His redeeming grace and love had cleansed my heart and His peace had filled my emptiness.

Chapter 25

Home at Last

Soon after I arrived in Evart, I started working at Kitchen Queen Stoves, where Alva worked. I learned to weld and do fabricating work, which I enjoyed for the most part. Up until now, my desire had been to become rich so I could prove to Wilbur Lee and my family that I could succeed. Now with my newfound faith I knew there was more to success than riches.

One day at lunch my boss called to me, "There's someone on the phone for you."

"Okay." I picked up the receiver, wondering who would be calling me here.

"Hello."

"Hello, Wil. This is Toby." The voice at the other end of the line sounded nervous.

"Toby!" I said, surprised. "How are you doing today?"

"I have a question for you." Toby wasted no time in small talk.

"Yes?" I said, not sure what to expect.

"Did you leave by your own choice, or did Wilbur Lee send you?" Toby asked.

"It was my choice, by the grace of God," I answered.

"Do you believe Wilbur Lee is right?"

"No."

"Do you think his prophecies will be fulfilled?"

"No."

"Are you planning to come back to the group?" Toby's question was pointed.

"No, absolutely not," I said. At this, Toby seemed to relax a bit.

"Where are you calling from?" I asked.

"I'm calling from a payphone in town. I just had to call you and ask you these questions. I hope it's all right that I made a collect call," he said apologetically.

"Oh, yes, that's no problem. We can talk as long as we want," I reassured him. "What's happening?"

"Ever since you left, Wilbur Lee has been telling us that you will come back to the group like you did the first time you left. He says you are away to tell more people about our beliefs, and when you come back you will bring more people to the group. I decided to call you and find out for myself. I'm calling from town so I won't raise any suspicion." Toby was opening up now. "I decided if you say that you *might* come back, Wilbur Lee is right, but if you say no, you won't come back, then Wilbur Lee is lying. I'm so sick of this," he finished.

"You are right about Wilbur Lee lying, because I never planned on coming back, and I'm certainly not gathering more people to join the group," I told him. I went on to tell him my experiences, and he shared his. "Would you feel ready to get away?" I finally asked.

"I'm not sure yet. I just don't want to do the wrong thing. I'll call you this afternoon if I decide to leave," he said.

"Okay. I'll be praying for you." With that, we hung up.

Later that afternoon my boss called me to the office and said the phone call was for me. I knew Toby had decided.

"Hello," I said.

"I am ready," Toby said. "I want you to pick me up tonight at midnight at the corner of State Road Nine and Two Hundred North."

"I'll be there," I promised.

That night I left with a friend, Gary. We got down to Indiana around eleven o'clock and stopped at a Pizza Hut to get a bite to eat before heading for the rendezvous. I relished the taste of pizza even more now than I had in the days before it had been forbidden.

We headed for the intersection but found it deserted. "Where is Toby?" I wondered aloud. There was no one in sight. "Let's turn around," I told Gary. He pulled off and turned around.

Suddenly I saw another vehicle pull up behind us. It was a police officer. "This is not what we need right now," I muttered. "Let's turn onto this side road," I suggested, hoping to shake off the officer. It didn't work. He drove up behind us and turned on his lights.

The officer walked up to Gary's open window. "Can I help you?" he asked. He was holding a long flashlight, beaming it in our faces.

"No, we are just waiting on someone," I explained,

hoping to satisfy him.

"It just appeared a bit suspicious." He spoke hesitantly.

"Oh, there he is," I said, pointing to Toby on his bicycle across the intersection. "It's my brother, and we are here to pick him up."

Without thinking, I opened the door and stepped outside. I realized my mistake when I saw the officer's hand flash to his revolver.

"Stay right where you are," he commanded. "I want to see your license." After checking our identification, he seemed satisfied and let us go.

Toby met us and we loaded his bicycle. He jumped into the pickup and we headed for Michigan. As we traveled, it seemed like old times again.

"So, what gave you second thoughts about Wilbur Lee?" I asked.

"You remember how he said that we will never die? All the people before our time have died, so how can we say that we will never die?" Toby asked.

"In Ecclesiastes it says there is a time to be born, and a time to die," I quoted.

"I still have a lot of questions," Toby added.

"Search the Scriptures. You can find your answers there." We shared more as we traveled north. It was 3:30 a.m. by the time we returned to Alva's house.

That morning before breakfast Toby asked, "May I use your phone, Alva? I'd like to call home to tell Mom and Dad where I am so they don't worry about me."

"Sure. That's a good idea," Alva agreed.

At the breakfast table, Toby related his call with Mom. "Mom picked up the phone and was surprised to hear me at the other end of the line. Since Indiana does not have daylight savings time, we're an hour ahead of them, so they were just getting up. She had no idea I was gone and thought I was still in bed."

"I'm glad you called before they realized you were gone," Alva said. "What did she say about you leaving?"

"She didn't say much," Toby continued. "I felt so sorry for hurting her. I explained that I no longer feel Wilbur Lee has the truth, and that is why I left.

"I also called Wilbur Lee. I wanted to tell him myself that I left." Toby had hardly touched the food on his plate. "He told us that if we ever think we are man enough to leave, we should be man enough to tell him, so I decided to call."

"What did you tell him?" I asked.

"I told him I don't feel comfortable with his teachings anymore and don't believe his way is the truth. I also told him if I don't find the truth anywhere else, I'll come back. He said he is persuaded that he has the truth, and someday I'll be back."

"The Bible says the truth will make you free," Alva said.

"That reminds me of something that happened a couple of months ago," Toby started in again. "I so longed to know what the truth is, I decided to pray. I felt guilty kneeling and praying, since we didn't usually address the Spirit this way. I prayed, 'If there is a true God out there and Wilbur Lee is wrong, please show me a way.' As I rose to my feet, an incredible peace enveloped me, and in my heart I knew that somewhere there is a truth that cannot be changed."

"God has shown you a way, hasn't He?" I pondered aloud.

"Yes, He has," Alva said confidently. "Let's pray and thank God for that."

As the weeks passed, Toby had many questions. We were able to identify with each other, and Alva helped us as we searched the Bible for answers.

One Sunday afternoon we were walking home from church. "Are you thinking of joining the church here?" Toby asked.

"I'm seriously considering it," I admitted. "They are pretty structured. It's kind of scary to be part of another group and extend trust again after the experience we had with Wilbur Lee."

"Yes, I know how you feel," Toby admitted. "I have been thinking of checking out some other types of churches, like the Protestants."

"Well, I did my share of visiting those types of churches after I broke away from Wilbur Lee," I cautioned. "I haven't found any churches that really practice complete biblical obedience, and they seem to have too much worldliness."

"Don't you think that if you join here, you will just be depending on the lifestyle to save you?" he questioned.

"No. I believe the church here has sound teaching and practices biblical principles. Alva and I have had many sincere discussions on living out our convictions. I am not just speaking about personal preferences, but convictions that are based on Bible principles. I would rather do without the conveniences of the more worldly churches and submit myself to the security of a biblical brotherhood that teaches and practices the whole Bible," I confided.

"But how do we know we are not just being drawn to another leader and his group?"

"I am confident that if I belong to a church that practices the whole Bible and doesn't take out a few things here and there like Wilbur Lee did, then I am safe. We must put our confidence in God, not in man. For now, I believe this is where God wants me, and I am committed to stay in His will. I don't think this is the only true church, but I believe it is a true church that follows God's teachings.

When a leader or group believes it is the only right one out there, then you can be sure there is a cult in the making. Perhaps they may not admit it, but they insinuate it by isolating themselves from other Bible-believing churches. Remember, we are to be a light to the world, the salt of the earth. How can we be this when we isolate ourselves?" I responded.

"You have given me a lot to think about. I have a lot to learn yet. According to what you are saying, we cannot just be born again and go on living independently; we must also commit ourselves to a spiritually sound brotherhood. Is that right?"

"That's exactly right, Toby. Giving Christ our whole heart means trusting Him with our fears of cults too. He will protect us if we stay in His will. I don't believe that a restricted lifestyle and practicing certain traditions are wrong as long as they don't violate Bible principles. Being open, loving each other, speaking the truth clearly and in love, and ministering to each other's needs, especially spiritual needs, are critical elements in a church. This is what I am looking for. I believe that is really what Wilbur

Lee's whole group was longing for. Wilbur Lee pretended to give it, but his motivations were selfish, and he destroyed us in the process. Many things happened that I may never understand, but I have put my trust in Jesus to supply what I really need."

We finished our walk home in quiet meditation.

* * *

Some time later at a funeral, I was surprised to see Jake Bontrager, our former Amish bishop. My heart skipped a beat. *I wonder if he remembers what he told Mom and Dad when they were excommunicated? I think I'll just ask him.*

I walked up and introduced myself. Jake was genuinely friendly and seemed pleased to meet me. After a few pleasantries, I brought up the subject. "Uh, I just wondered if you remember a statement you made to Mom, Dad, and Carolyn. We understood that you said you will *meit uns bist da blut rot shamt!*" (Shun us till the red blood froths!) I held my breath, waiting on his reaction.

Bishop Jake slowly stroked his long white beard, his face puzzled. "I simply can't remember saying anything like that." He shook his head. "I do remember quoting a Scripture verse in German concerning the *meiting* (shunning) that could sound similar toward the end. '*So aber jemand nicht gehorsam ist unserm Wort, den zeiget an durch einen Brief, und habt nicht mit ihm zu schaffen, auf das er schamrot werde.*' " (And if any man obey not our word by this epistle, note that man, and have no company with him, that he may be ashamed. 2 Thessalonians 3:14.)

My mouth dropped open. "So they misunderstood you?" I could hardly believe it. All these years we had nursed a grudge upon a misunderstanding. "Well, I'm sure glad to have that cleared up!" I exclaimed.

That evening my thoughts traveled back to the conversation with Bishop Jake. I was sobered when I realized how easily my parents had misunderstood the last part of the verse to mean something completely different. It was also sobering to realize how easily, if not eagerly, the group had believed the error. I shook my head sadly. What a lesson! I knew now that the ministry was acting out of love, doing the best they knew. On the other hand, I couldn't help but wonder if some things couldn't have been handled differently. Could there have been more dialogue? More explanation? Maybe that would have made a difference, especially since Dad couldn't hear well.

My thoughts ran deep as I pondered. There were things about the cult I would never understand. But I knew we had made wrong choices, and we were responsible for them. We should have been more open, more charitable toward the ministry, and more teachable. We should have been more cautious with Wilbur Lee, more discerning, much wiser. On the other hand, I wondered what we could learn from this. Could we do some things differently as a church to be able to help more? I was no longer part of the cult. I was outside looking in. What would I do when I saw my brothers and sisters in Christ leaning in that direction, being lured by false teaching?

We were wrong, no doubt, and very foolish, I thought. We had hurt the church and our families much more than they had hurt us. However, we also had some deep-seated motives that were not easily detected on the surface. We were part of the Amish church community. We were living according to the guidelines, yet our hearts were far from God, completely out of His will. We were lonely, longing for fulfillment, for understanding and compassion. We wanted healing for our hurts. We were thirsty, empty, and longing for satisfaction in life. We were searching for security, for direction, for the filling of the Holy Spirit.

We were filled with a spirit, but the wrong one. We found answers, but the wrong ones. We found understanding and security, but they were short-lived. We drank of a spring, though contaminated, and our thirst increased, our void deepened.

I sighed deeply, and Alva looked up from the book he was reading.

"Is something wrong?" he asked.

I smiled thoughtfully and shook my head. Wrong? The true Father had led me to the right answers and filled me with His Spirit. I'd been lost, but now was found. Blind, but now could see. Dead, but was now alive. My heart welled up with gratitude toward the Savior who loved me enough to rescue me.

"No, nothing's wrong," I finally answered, meeting my brother's questioning gaze. "At last, something is right."

Epilogue

Grace be to you and peace from God our Father, and from the Lord Jesus Christ. Blessed be God, even the Father of our Lord Jesus Christ, the Father of mercies, and the God of all comfort; who comforteth us in all our tribulation, that we may be able to comfort them which are in any trouble, by the comfort wherewith we ourselves are comforted of God.
— *2 Corinthians 1:2-4*

This verse means a lot to me. It brings out who God, the true Father, really is. God has given me peace and comfort. In return, I want to let God use me to bring comfort to others, but God alone can give you true peace.

God has been very good to me. I don't deserve the many blessings He has given me, but I'm thankful for them. In September of 1995, with a joyful heart, I was baptized and became a member of the Evart Amish church. Two years after coming to Evart, I married a wonderful woman, Joann, daughter of Omer and Martha Miller. Our wedding day, June 12, 1997, was a beautiful, sunny day.

Not all of my family attended, but we were thankful for the ones who did come. We have been blessed with four healthy children—one daughter, Janice Lorine, and three sons, Jeffrey Omer, Jaylin James, and Justin Daniel.

Toby was married in September of the same year to Carol Gingerich. They have been blessed with six healthy children. They reside in Manton, Michigan, and are also members of the Amish church.

My sister Elsie and her husband Monroe brought their family to Evart, Michigan, in 1994. They had been there almost a year before I arrived at Alva's. Elsie was still struggling to know if Wilbur Lee was right or not. After I shared my story, she understood that Wilbur Lee had deceived them.

Some time after I had moved out of Holland, the rest of the families who were still with the group all moved up to Holland to the apartment complex where we had been renting. Every household then bought their own apartment.

In 1995 Manass and Wilma were also enlightened. They came up to visit one Sunday afternoon, much to our surprise. They had many questions, and we were able to help them see where they had been deceived. Praise the Lord!

As the years went by, I watched another young boy move in with Wilbur Lee. He soon became disgusted with the living arrangement and moved out. It was not long until another young adolescent boy moved into Wilbur Lee's apartment. This was almost more than I could bear. I confronted Wilbur Lee. He denied that anything inappropriate was happening. After much praying for guidance and much discussion with other former cult members, we decided to report him to the government authorities.

In early August of 2002, another former cult member and I went to the Holland Police Department and filed a report. They did some detective work and found evidence to support our claims. On August 23 Wilbur Lee Eash was arrested and charged with first-degree criminal sexual conduct. He later pleaded guilty to a less serious charge. On March 7, 2003, he received a twenty-month to fifteen-year prison sentence. He would serve a minimum of twenty months before being eligible for parole. As of this writing, he is still in prison.

After Wilbur Lee was imprisoned, more of his followers broke away and no longer adhered to his teachings.

In late June of 2008 we received word that Dad (Clarence Hochstetler) was very ill and in the hospital. We children got to visit with him before he died on July 8 at the age of seventy-eight. The day before he died, test results revealed that he had cancer. In respect of his wishes, we limited the funeral to family members. His final resting place is in Pilgrim Home Cemetery in Holland, Michigan. We all miss his presence.

Sometimes bad things happen to people, but when we give our wounds to God, He can take them and make something beautiful out of them. I give this story to God for Him to use as He pleases.

— Wilbur Hochstetler

June 2010

Appendix

Characteristics of a Cult

*Beloved, believe not every spirit, but try
the spirits whether they are of God: because many
false prophets are gone out into the world. — 1 John 4:1*

In a cult, one person controls and dictates a group's beliefs and actions. Members are not free to question the doctrines or the system. Any religious movement that claims the backing of the Bible but distorts the central message of Christianity either through new revelation or by replacing a biblical principle with a deviation of their own interpretation is a cult.

The Webster's Dictionary defines a cult as "a quasi-religious group, often living in a colony, with a charismatic leader who indoctrinates members with unorthodox or extremist views, practices, or beliefs; a devoted attachment to, or extravagant admiration for, a person, principle, or lifestyle, especially when regarded as a fad (definitions 1b and 2a).

There are a number of characteristics you almost always see in cults.

1) The leader is usually in control of the money. He says the money is used for a greater purpose in the group or society at large, yet he himself largely benefits from it.

2) He demands strict obedience to him; he craves power. Anyone who raises questions is considered a threat.

3) He is uncannily interested in the private lives of his followers; for example, arranging marriages, demanding celibacy, or even regulating what kind of underwear his followers wear. Often he is sexually involved with members of his group.

4) Occult activities such as divining or clairvoyance are commonly practiced by cult leaders. In our case, it was "communication with the spirit." The finger pressing was a form of divining in order to receive answers. Certain faith healing and other mysterious or magical powers are often used to maintain faith in the leader.

5) Cults always progress toward evil. The most prominent character we see is the one specifically described in 2 Timothy 3:13: "But evil men and seducers shall wax worse and worse, deceiving, and being deceived." Every cult starts out looking quite innocent, but cults always progress, never to the better, always to the worse. They claim they have the truth and no one else does. When that happens, beware.

How a Person Becomes Susceptible

People don't deliberately join cults; they join churches, special interest or self-help groups, and even multi-level marketing firms. All of these groups can be good, yet groups under these labels have ensnared people and controlled them to the point that they did not dare think for themselves. They succumbed to the leaders' mind control and believed their unrealistic promises.

Proverbs 29:18 says, "Where there is no vision, the people perish: but he that keepeth the law, happy is he." A person with no vision has no goals, no meaningful prayer life. He just does what is required of him without really understanding why. There is an emptiness he can't shake off or fulfill. He exists, but does not feel or see the Lord's purpose for his life, which often seems like a meaningless existence. In this state of mind or spiritual condition, a person does not have good judgment, because he has no solid foundation for his beliefs. His house is built upon the sand. He is open to deception.

Jesus said, "Take heed that no man deceive you" (Matthew 24:4). He warns us that there will be people who claim to be Christ. How do we keep from being deceived? In 2 Thessalonians 2:3 we read, "Let no man deceive you by any means: for that day shall not come, except there come a falling away first." This verse brings the responsibility home to us. When we harbor ill feelings such as bitterness, rebellion, contempt, anger, and resentment, we are falling away. When we do not repent of a sin in our life, we deceive ourselves. First John 1:8 says, "If we say that we have no sin, we deceive ourselves, and the truth is not in us."

A person who is deceived is ignoring the truth. Any person who holds writings such as the Book of Mormon, a deviant Bible translation (such as the Jehovah's Witness Bible), or even the Apocrypha equal to or above the Bible is susceptible to deception. God made the truth, which is the Bible, available to us; we just need to receive it and believe it. When Eve was deceived, it wasn't that she didn't know the truth. She was made to believe that if she ate the forbidden fruit she would gain the knowledge of good and evil and become as gods. It is interesting to note that she already knew what good was, but Satan made her believe God was withholding something from her by not letting her know what evil was. Had she adhered to the truth as God had said, "Ye shall not eat of it, neither shall ye touch it, lest ye die," she would not have become deceived.

Let's return to the age-old question Pilot asked Jesus: "What is truth?" Often, as with Eve, the truth is no longer clear. It has been twisted until what God has said does not seem like the truth anymore. In our case, we depended on our Amish lifestyle to save us instead of immersing ourselves in the Word. Therefore we were not grounded in the truth. Had we studied God's word, we would have known from Romans 16:18 that those who come with "good words and fair speeches deceive the hearts of the simple." Had we studied the whole verse, we could have seen that those who serve themselves are not in the truth.

Had we greater knowledge of the Scriptures, we would have been able to detect the lies and inconsistencies in our leader's teachings. We would have known that we "know neither the day nor the hour wherein the Son of man cometh" (Matthew 25:13), for "of that day and that hour knoweth no man, no, not the angels which are in heaven, neither the Son, but the Father" (Mark 13:32), and so not been led astray by his false predictions of the end. We would have understood that "all scripture is given by inspiration of God" (2 Timothy 3:16) and not been susceptible to our leader's claims that parts were intended to deceive. His erroneous teachings concerning marriage, money, the roles of women, and communicating with spirits would have been obvious to us had we only been more familiar with the Scriptures.

The Church's Responsibility

While we are in a fallen world, we will never be able to create a perfect environment where no one makes wrong choices. Does that leave the church free of any responsibility? No. When people desire to become members, they should be clearly taught what the new birth is. The new birth should be evident in their lives before they are allowed to become members. They should be taught what it means to live a Christ-like life and how to have a meaningful prayer life. God's will is that we portray His image and be part of His kingdom (the church) on this earth. But how can the church teach these things if it does not understand the new birth? How can it demonstrate Christ-likeness when its members show anger, resentment, and bitterness? How can it be His image when sin is allowed in the church? When these things are present in the church, there is work to be done.

The Bible talks a lot about how to deal with sin in the church, which I won't address here. Besides discipline, the church needs to give sound biblical teaching. This responsibility lies with all members, but especially with the ministers.

All members should look to the spiritual welfare of the other members. "He that loveth his brother abideth in the light, and there is none occasion of stumbling in him" (1 John 2:10). If we really analyze what this verse is saying, it is quite serious. There is *none*—not even *one*—occasion of stumbling in him that abideth in the light and loveth his brother. So we must conclude that when we have been a stumbling block to our brother, we weren't walking in the light or loving him. Inconsistencies such as professing Christianity but living a non-Christ-like life cause big stumbling blocks.

When the church does not deal with sins of the heart or even blatant sins, its members become disillusioned. Members also become disillusioned when the church resorts to tradition rather than giving sound biblical teaching. The members do not see the need to live an upright life. Being a church member becomes just a form, a way of life, rather than a meaningful relationship with the Lord and His people.

Often in this environment a person will start to search for meaning in life, which is good. But when he starts to ask questions he is looked at as odd or rebellious. Sadly, in some plain churches questions are squelched with the reasoning that the person is seeking for more material things, thus creating a cultic environment where one is not free to ask questions. When that happens he is pushed to live a meaningless life, a life without a vision. The church should be there to foster that search and direct it to Christ.

Seeking Freedom

If you find yourself in a cult or in an environment where you have no one to turn to for advice or help, first seek God's guidance. Pray. "And I say unto you, Ask, and it shall be given you; seek, and ye shall find; knock, and it shall be opened unto you" (Luke 11:9). Find a Bible and read it. Earnestly seek the truth.

Look for an opportunity to speak with a person you know could help you out of your situation. Make sure he understands the dire circumstance you are in and that you need to get out *now*.

Once you are away from your situation, seek spiritual counseling and become grounded in the truth. Until you are completely grounded in the truth, do not trust yourself to speak alone with any members of your former group.

For those of you who have family or know someone who is involved with a cult, my heart goes out to you. What can you do? First of all, pray. There is power in prayer. "The effectual fervent prayer of a righteous man availeth much" (James 5:16). Get the whole church to pray for the situation. Not only does it activate God's power in the situation, it puts you in the right frame of mind, which is very important. Sometimes people, when trying to help, respond out of fear and therefore come across as angry and frustrated, which only convinces the person in the cult that people outside it are bad. You have to build up trust and befriend him. Visit often and take an honest interest in his life.

In order to help someone, it is of utmost importance that you are grounded in the truth of the Bible and are filled with the Holy Spirit. Then when you are questioned you will be able to give sound teaching. Otherwise, you are in danger of becoming deceived yourself. Always make yourself accountable to the church so if you become disillusioned they will immediately be able to correct you.

Remember you cannot help someone who does not want to be helped. Just be there for him and plant seeds of Bible truth and let God do His work. Then if there comes a time when he starts to question the cult, he will have someone to turn to for help. May God bless you in your endeavor.

— Wilbur Hochstetler

Additional Recommended Reading:

The Cults and the Occult
by: Edmund C. Gruss
Available from:
Ridgeway Books
3129 Fruit Ave
Medina, NY 14103
585.798.0050

About the Author

Nathan and his wife Mattie live in rural Michigan with their three daughters, Sharon Marie, Martha Sue, and Emilee Hope. They are members of the Evart Amish Church. Nathan is a brother-in-law to Wilbur Hochstetler, the book's main character. He enjoys writing and spending time with his family and is a partner at Dyna Products, a firewood-processing equipment manufacturer. This is his first book.